THE EXTRACTIONIST

ALSO BY MICHAELA JEFFERY

WROL (Without Rule of Law)

THE EXTRACTIONIST

MICHAELA JEFFERY

PLAYWRIGHTS CANADA PRESS
TORONTO

First edition: March 2025
Printed and bound in Canada by Imprimerie Gauvin Ltée, Gatineau

Jacket art and design by Nick Johnson

Playwrights Canada Press
202-269 Richmond St. W., Toronto, ON M5V 1X1
416.703.0013 | info@playwrightscanada.com | www.playwrightscanada.com

LIBRARY AND ARCHIVES CANADA CATALOGUING IN PUBLICATION
Title: The extractionist / Michaela Jeffery.
Names: Jeffery, Michaela, author
Description: First edition.
Identifiers: Canadiana (print) 20240532163 | Canadiana (ebook) 20240533003 | ISBN 9780369105394 (softcover) | ISBN 9780369105400 (PDF) | ISBN 9780369105417 (EPUB)
Subjects: LCGFT: Drama.
Classification: LCC PS8619.E4446 E98 2025 | DDC C812/.6—dc23

Playwrights Canada Press staff work across Turtle Island, on Treaty 13 and Treaty 20 territories, as well as unceded lands, which are the current, ancestral, and future homes of the Anishinaabe Nations (Ojibwe / Chippewa, Odawa, Potawatomi, Algonquin, Saulteaux, Nipissing, and Mississauga / Michi Saagiig), the Wendat, members of the Haudenosaunee Confederacy (Mohawk, Oneida, Onondaga, Cayuga, Seneca, and Tuscarora), and the xʷməθkʷəy̓əm (Musqueam), Sḵwx̱wú7mesh (Squamish), and səlilwətaɬ (Tsleil-Waututh) Nations, as well as Metis and Inuit peoples. It always was and always will be Indigenous land.

We acknowledge the financial support of the Canada Council for the Arts, the Ontario Arts Council (OAC), Ontario Creates, the Government of Ontario, and the Government of Canada for our publishing activities.

This story is for my mother, my stepmother, and my sisters. It is for anyone that has ever found themselves in a place where they knew staying down would be safer than going another round but chose to get up and swing again anyway.

FOREWORD

What kind of heroes do we need in a rapidly changing world full of unseen enemies? More importantly, what kind of hero are you willing to trust in a time when societal pillars like truth and justice seem subjective. If your hero is blocked in their noble pursuit by those same pillars, is it okay if they simply go around them, or even topple them to the ground? To save us from this uncomfortable moral conundrum, perhaps the kind of hero we need today is one that we don't recognize or even see coming. One who acts before we fully understand what they are intending and departs before we can think too deeply on their motivations. Thank you, Michaela, for creating the exact kind of hero that we need right now, in all her complexity. I can't wait for more adventures!

Craig Hall
Director

AUTHOR'S NOTES

"Nobody wakes up and thinks, today I'm going to join a cult."

Thank you for picking up this copy of *The Extractionist*. This play was developed and premiered at Vertigo Theatre (Calgary, AB). In my original commission pitch—before I knew the full shape of the story I wanted to write—I talked about my lifelong love of classic mysteries. I talked about being an avid consumer of Dashiell Hammett, Agatha Christie, and Sir Arthur Conan Doyle. I said I wanted to create a story that was as large and lush—with a mystery as twisty and satisfying—as those I'd grown up admiring.

I also knew that I wanted this story to be anchored with a different kind of protagonist. I was riveted by the intricacy and the moral complexities of the contemporary characters that drove stories like *Broadchurch*, *Mare of Easttown*, and *Sharp Objects*. I'd learned quickly that my favourite sort of protagonist is an unsettled one—someone whom we're perhaps not completely sure we can trust.

Asha is this sort of hero—a figure whose motives are always her own, and whose complicated morality maybe gives us pause. Her actions raise difficult questions: In a society where the forces of law and order are intrinsically tied to privilege and power, what is the cost of justice and to what lengths would it be reasonable to go in its pursuit?

The world of this play is a dynamic, immersive, evolving landscape that is populated by a collection of distinct characters who, like Asha, each hold their own values, allegiances, fears, and motivations: Its heroes don't play by the rules and its villains don't stalk the shadows—they host alt-right podcasts.

The Extractionist was commissioned and developed by Vertigo Theatre and was first produced by Vertigo at the Playhouse, Calgary, from January 28 to February 26, 2023, with the following cast and creative team:

Reuben Medina: Mike Tan
Kate / Officer Lena Romero: Vanessa Leticia Jetté
Asha Ray: Monice Peter
Grant Langdon / Paul Kelly: Robert Klein
Detective Alison Beechum / Luminia Receptionist: Tara Beagan
Matt Langdon / Franco / IT Guy: Joe Perry
Richard Holland / Serge: Stafford Perry
Understudies: Emily Howard and Eric Wigston

Director: Craig Hall
Assistant Director: Caleigh Crow
Set and Projection Design: Andy Moro
Costume Design: Deitra Kalyn
Lighting Design: Narda McCarroll
Original Composition: Malcolm Dow
Additional Composition: Torquil Campbell
Sound Design: Thomas Geddes
Assistant Set and Projection Design: Anna Shepard
Fight/Intimacy Director: Brianna Johnston
Stage Manager: Laurel O'Neil
Assistant Stage Manager: Ashley Rees
Apprentice Stage Manager: Millie Winzinowich
Playwriting Mentee: Cayley Wreggitt

CHARACTERS (IN ORDER OF APPEARANCE)

Reuben Medina (40s, M)
Asha Ray (30s, F)
Kate (20s, F)
Grant Langdon (60s, M)
Detective Alison Beechum (30s, F)
Matt Langdon (20s, M)
Richard Holland (60s, M)

SPEAKING OTHERS

Franco
Paul Kelly
Officer Lena Romero
Serge "The Russian"
Maya Ruiz

NON-SPEAKING OTHERS

Luminia Receptionist
IT Guy

PROPOSED DOUBLING

Reuben Medina
Asha Ray
Kate / Officer Lena Romero / Maya Ruiz
Grant Langdon / Paul Kelly
Richard Holland / Serge "The Russian"
Alison Beechum / Luminia Receptionist
Matt Langdon / Franco / IT Guy

ACT ONE

SCENE ONE

Night. A large metropolis. It rains heavily. Reuben MEDINA *puts up the collar of his jacket, walking faster. The dark street is a wash of liquid neon, wet asphalt reflecting flickering billboards. He is moving quickly, short of breath—the feeling of weaving down crowded city streets. He grips his phone to his ear. He leaves a message.*

MEDINA: Hey, it's me.
Again.
Look, I get it—you don't want to see my face.
Fine.

But.
This kid, Asha . . .

A slight pause.

It's . . . slippery as hell.

A slight pause.

I've run this thing up every chain of command in three jurisdictions and I am nowhere.

I am—

He looks over his shoulder, uneasy.

. . . stonewalled to hell. Makes me think—

He looks over his shoulder again.

I don't know. I don't know what to think.

Silence. He makes the decision.

I'm going to come by your place.

Just take a look, yeah?
Tell me what I'm not seeing.

He hangs up. He raises his hand to flag a cab. He is swallowed into the throng of the city.

SCENE TWO (A)

The Clairmont—a shitty diner named for a fancy hotel. It's unremarkable. Dated. Peeling vinyl booths and worn linoleum. A pie carousel. The smell of gravy and burnt coffee. Unforgiving lights. The rain outside is coming down heavily. The city beyond is wet and glossy—pulsing, harried. The roar and slosh of heavy traffic. The hissing of buses. The rumble of subway trains deep underground. Inside the diner it's muggy and eerily still. The sole patron, ASHA *Ray, sits alone in a booth, nursing a coffee. She gazes out through the fogged window into the darkness beyond. The server,* KATE, *approaches. She wears a diner uniform, complete with capped sleeves and name badge. She freshens* ASHA*'s coffee.*

KATE: You want anything else?

ASHA: I'm fine.

KATE: Soup of the day is decent. And there's biscuits.

ASHA: Just the coffee.

KATE: Okay.

KATE *hesitates.*

Let me know. If you change your mind.

ASHA *nods.* KATE *lingers at her table. She follows* ASHA*'s gaze out into the dark night.*

I hate it.

ASHA looks at her.

When it's so dark out there and so bright in here, I mean. Always feels like someone's looking in.

They both look back out through the fogged glass into the darkness beyond.

A moment of tense stillness.

A bus horn blares loudly.

KATE fumbles the coffee carafe she's still holding, almost dropping it, sloshing coffee across the table.

Shit. Sorry.

ASHA pulls a wad of napkins from the metal holder and mops the spill.

ASHA: Don't worry about it.

KATE: *(wryly)* I'm new here.

They smile at each other.

KATE wipes the underside of the table and opposite bench with a bar rag.

ASHA checks her watch.

Looks like you're getting stood up.

ASHA: Let's hope not.

ASHA smiles again, but KATE has gone somber.

KATE resumes wiping the bench.

ASHA piles up the wadded-up napkins beside the condiment caddy.

The Clairmont's front door opens with a whine and a bang, setting the bobbleheads on the countertop dancing.

Grant LANGDON enters, sopping wet and agitated. He looks weary—older than his years. He is attired in the way a wealthy person might imagine appears inconspicuous. It is not. He exudes status and impatience.

LANGDON scans the small space, spotting ASHA. He moves briskly to her booth. When he reaches it, he stalls, suddenly uncharacteristically hesitant.

LANGDON: Asha Ray?

She nods. LANGDON looks around, then awkwardly slides into the booth across from her.

ASHA: What can I do for you, Mr. Langdon?

He says nothing. He runs a hand through his tousled grey hair. He looks intently at ASHA. His gaze travels to the stack of soggy napkins. The rotating pie carousel. He seems to take in his surroundings for the first time since arriving.

LANGDON: I'm not sure.

ASHA looks at him.

ASHA: You expressed on the phone that it was urgent.

LANGDON seems to snap back to the present.

LANGDON: Yes, yes. I—

He stops himself.

LANGDON: I thought this would be an office. This address.

Pause.

I've lived in this city my whole life. I didn't know this place existed.

ASHA: Would you prefer an office?

LANGDON: Pardon?

ASHA: It seems to me like you'd prefer to disclose your concerns to someone with an office.

LANGDON: No. It's not important. You were recommended.

ASHA: By whom?

LANGDON: Private investigator. Name of Paul Kelly. Says you're . . . effective.

ASHA: At what?

LANGDON shifts, uneasy. He glances at KATE behind the service counter, brewing a fresh pot of coffee.

LANGDON: Look. I just want my kid back.

ASHA: Your kid?

LANGDON: My son. Matt.

ASHA: Where is he?

LANGDON: He didn't do this. He didn't. I know my kid.

ASHA: Mr. Langdon. Where is Matt?

LANGDON deflates. He rubs his face.

LANGDON: He was . . . detained.

ASHA: If Matt is in police custody, you need a lawyer, not a deprogrammer.

LANGDON: I have a lawyer. I have a whole stable of lawyers telling me that they can't do a goddamned thing. He's refused counsel.

ASHA: And you think I can help?

LANGDON: He won't see me.

ASHA: Why not?

LANGDON appears to deflate again.

LANGDON: I don't know. He needs to speak with a lawyer—

ASHA: Mr. Langdon, I'm not sure how Paul Kelly explained what I do—

LANGDON: Gets them back. He said: She gets them back.

He looks at her intently again. She returns his gaze evenly.

ASHA: I work with families. I locate and isolate individuals who need assistance removing themselves from their . . . circumstance.

LANGDON: Cults.

ASHA: Sometimes. Do you believe that's what's happening with Matt?

> *LANGDON doesn't say what he believes. He looks away. He is ashamed of his son—it's palpable. He takes a breath, perhaps unsure where to start.*

LANGDON: He's not a . . . soft . . . kid. He's smart. Confident.

ASHA: How old is he?

LANGDON: Twenty-six. A recent graduate—MBA from SRU Tech.

ASHA: Are you close?

> *Pause.*

LANGDON: No.

> *Pause.*

ASHA: Does Matt have . . . anyone else? Other family? Friends?

> *LANGDON shakes his head, uncertain.*

Does he work?

> *LANGDON looks right at her.*

LANGDON: He runs marketing analytics for a policy institute. A think tank.

They have a campus in Capitol Point.

He's living there. It's a whole
Community
Other young people
I thought—
He seemed . . . focused. Motivated.

I didn't know.

ASHA watches him.

He put his "advisor" as his next of kin.
I wasn't notified—when they brought him in.
He didn't call me. Or his mother. He called his employer.
What does that suggest to you?

ASHA: Why was Matt detained?

LANGDON looks at his hands.

LANGDON: There's . . . a girl missing.

ASHA: Missing?

LANGDON: She—
Someone he was . . . involved with.
The police think that my son . . .

LANGDON hesitates.

. . . that he has knowledge of her disappearance.

Silence.

Matty is a varsity athlete for God's sake.
Disciplined. Conscientious.

An accusation like this . . .
It will follow to him the rest of his life.

She stares down at her coffee.

ASHA: You want me to speak with him?

LANGDON: Yes.

ASHA: I don't know if that will be possible.

LANGDON: I can pay.

ASHA: It's a question of access.

LANGDON: Paul Kelly said you're the best. That you'll do what needs to be done. That you are able to work around legal obstacles—

ASHA: Matt is in police custody. If he's released—

LANGDON: No. I want him out. Now. I want him to meet with a lawyer.

ASHA: I understand that, Mr. Langdon.

LANGDON: They won't protect him. Those people.

Silence.

ASHA: You suggested Matt is only willing to speak with his "advisor." Do you know who that is?

LANGDON shakes his head. ASHA stirs her coffee.

This organization—

LANGDON: Luminia.

ASHA stops stirring her coffee.

ASHA: Luminia. What do you know about it?

LANGDON: It's a . . . research firm, essentially, I believe. They advise on governmental policy . . . mostly economic strategy. It's run by a retired professor from a California university—a public speaker.

Beat.

ASHA: Richard Holland.

Beat.

LANGDON: Yes.

ASHA nods. She sits back.

ASHA: What about the girl? Is she involved?

LANGDON: I don't know.

ASHA: What does Paul Kelly think?

LANGDON: Kelly?

ASHA: You hired him to find her, right?

LANGDON says nothing. He looks at his hands again.

You're hoping he locates her before the police.

LANGDON: I just—want to be kept appraised.

She looks at him for a long moment.

ASHA: And if he turns up evidence that implicates Matt?

LANGDON: Do you have children?

ASHA: No.

LANGDON looks at his hands.

LANGDON: I'll protect my son.

Silence. There is only the quiet hum of radiators, and the squeak of KATE's cloth as she wipes the already spotless service counter for the third time.

ASHA: Did you try to pay him?

LANGDON: Who?

ASHA: Holland.

A lengthy silence. LANGDON deliberates what to say. He settles on honesty.

LANGDON: I told that bastard I'd write him a cheque on the spot—half a million dollars—to cut Matty loose, to let me handle his defence.

You know what that asshole says? Says no. Says it's a matter of "moral principle"—that Matty is "demonstrating his commitment" to his Luminia family. *(rubbing his face again)* Son of a bitch.

Silence.

ASHA: I'll do what I can, Mr. Langdon. And I'll keep you appraised.

Silence.

LANGDON: Thank you.

They lapse into silence. Neither moves to leave. ASHA looks into her coffee cup.

ASHA: . . . you said, "I'll protect my son."

LANGDON: Yes.

ASHA: Even if he's responsible . . . for what might have happened to that girl?

LANGDON seems to age under the weight of the question.

LANGDON: He's my son.

The statement hangs. LANGDON rubs his face again. It's evident he's weeping. ASHA looks at KATE, who has finally stopped cleaning the counter—KATE's expression is stony, unreadable. She gives ASHA the slightest hint of a nod. ASHA reaches out her hand and places it over LANGDON's—a gesture of comfort.

The Clairmont's lights flicker. The rumble of the subway trains below rattles the cutlery. Dark shapes are visible out beyond the glass of the window—hundreds of thousands of commuters.

SCENE TWO (B)

A single illuminated desk in the police precinct. Detective Alison BEECHUM stands, flipping through pages in a file. She glances up at her desk phone, then back to the file. She glances up at the phone again. She picks it up like she intends to make a call. She hesitates. She puts the phone down. A uniformed officer—Officer Lena ROMERO*—appears in the doorway. She nods to* BEECHUM. BEECHUM *collects the folder from her desk, as well as her cold mug of coffee. She follows* ROMERO *out, turning out the lights.*

Outside it rains harder.

SCENE THREE

The street in front of ASHA*'s apartment building. She approaches in a hurry; the hood of her jacket is pulled up against the weather. She doesn't notice the man loitering under the awning. She digs her keys from her pocket.*

MEDINA *steps toward her from the dark entryway.*

MEDINA: Asha.

She starts.

ASHA: Jesus Christ.

She looks up at him. Astonished. Annoyed. She takes a step back.

What are you doing here?

MEDINA: I called. A dozen times. You didn't pick up.

ASHA: So, you came to my apartment?

MEDINA: You didn't pick up.

ASHA: I don't want to talk to you.

MEDINA: Yeah, I got it. Look—

ASHA: Get out of here, Medina.

MEDINA: Ten minutes. Let me run this thing down for you, then I'm gone.

ASHA: No.

MEDINA: Ten minutes.

ASHA: I'm not interested.

MEDINA: Personal favour.

ASHA: You're out of those. Move.

She tries to get past him. MEDINA *stands his ground.*

MEDINA: Look, I've got a job for you.

ASHA: I'm already working a job. Too many jobs.

MEDINA: I need intel—I need whatever you can get me on a guy who runs a "change your life" business school out of Capitol Point.

ASHA stills.

ASHA: What's this about?

He takes a step toward her.

MEDINA: Ten minutes.

He lifts the parcel he's had concealed under his arm. It's beer. *ASHA regards him intently. Finally, she relents. She opens the door.*

ASHA: Wipe your feet.

He follows her inside. She stops and looks up at him again in the light of the cramped entryway. Their bodies are close, almost touching. The air is charged.

You look like hell.

MEDINA: Thanks.

She reaches around him and collects her mail.

ASHA: Ten minutes.

He holds the interior door for her and follows her up the derelict stairwell toward her apartment.

MEDINA: Nice place.

ASHA: Fuck you.

MEDINA: It has character.

ASHA: I'm doing you a favour.

MEDINA: Why are you living here?

ASHA: Excuse me?

MEDINA: Seems like, with all these private commissions you got now, you could rent yourself someplace without needles in the stairwell.

ASHA: There's a waitlist for the penthouse at the Royal George.

MEDINA: I'm serious.

ASHA: Miss your badge?

MEDINA: That's not—I'm just saying—

ASHA: Saying what?

MEDINA: You make a lot of enemies. Should think about living someplace where your neighbours don't leave the building door propped open with a brick when they go out to smoke.

They come to an abrupt halt on the landing outside ASHA*'s apartment. The door is ajar. The frame is splintered. It's evident that the door has been kicked in—an act of considerable violence. It feels genuinely chilling.* MEDINA *fixes* ASHA *with a look that clearly says "wait here"—knowing she won't. He pushes on the door. It swings open into the dark apartment. The silence buzzes around them. He moves with noiseless efficiency, performing a sweep of the space.* MEDINA *was a cop for many years, and it shows.* ASHA *picks up the wooden bat she's left leaning near the door.* MEDINA *quickly completes his sweep: Whoever has been here is long gone.*

It's clear.

ASHA *switches on the light. The place is modest, sparse, disordered. Takeout boxes are piled up by the trash. A threadbare sofa. A punching bag suspended from the living room ceiling. A dead fern on the window overlooking the alley. The place appears to have been searched. Cabinets hang open, papers are strewn across the floor.* ASHA *puts the bat back by the door, she drops her purse and keys on the counter.* MEDINA *inspects the splintered door jamb.* ASHA *opens the fridge and grabs a couple beers, the same kind* MEDINA *brought.*

You gonna call this in?

ASHA: No. No uniforms.

MEDINA: Asha.

ASHA: Don't.

MEDINA: What?

ASHA: Get up my ass about this.

MEDINA stares at her in disbelief.

MEDINA: You got a theory?

ASHA: On what?

MEDINA: On who kicked in your goddamned door.

ASHA cracks her beer.

ASHA: No. You want one?

She offers him the second beer. He looks at her for a long moment. He takes it.

MEDINA: Jesus.

ASHA: You're down to eight minutes.

He crosses his arms.

MEDINA: What if the guy comes back?

ASHA: You were on the job sixteen years. How often did you see someone toss a place, leave, and then come back later?

MEDINA: You know what they were after?

ASHA: No.

MEDINA: And you wouldn't tell me if you did.

ASHA: Correct.

MEDINA fights to get a handle on his frustration.

MEDINA: You could stay at Gamma House.

ASHA: No. Thanks.

MEDINA: It's safe. It's anonymous—

ASHA: Medina, no offence but I'll take my chances. I'm not going to bunk with a bunch of kids at your halfway house.

Now what can I do for you?

MEDINA looks at her.

MEDINA: Richard Holland.

ASHA: What about him?

MEDINA: What do you know about his operation?

ASHA: Luminia?

MEDINA: Yeah. What is it?

ASHA: On paper, it's a policy institute.

MEDINA: In practice?

She peels the label from her beer.

ASHA: Holland is a predator.

MEDINA watches her closely.

MEDINA: He's faculty over at SRU.

ASHA: Not anymore. He does seminars. Sells out arenas. "Realize your potential" kind of shit.

MEDINA: Huh. And how exactly does one realize their potential?

ASHA smiles, faintly. This makes MEDINA feel good.

ASHA: His product is leadership courses. Offered by Luminia out of their campus in Capitol Point.

MEDINA: What's the draw?

ASHA looks at him. She realizes he's picked up on the depth of her interest in the subject of Richard Holland.

ASHA: It may surprise you to know, I don't have comprehensive profiles worked up detailing the individual MOs of every creep out there cultivating a following.

MEDINA: Yeah, but you know this one well enough.

ASHA: How do you figure that?

MEDINA: Come on, Asha. What do you have for me?

Something simmers between them.

ASHA: This isn't his first rodeo, Holland.

MEDINA: Meaning?

ASHA: Meaning the guy's had practice.

MEDINA: Where?

ASHA: Here's my recommendation: Have your cop buddies look into businesses Holland's been connected to before Luminia. I'm sure it'll be informative. Maybe they'll get lucky and find something they can charge him with.

MEDINA: I'm not here on behalf of the police, and I'm not after Holland. I'm looking for someone. A kid. I've been calling you about it for a couple weeks. She's shacked up with a Luminia member—

ASHA: Shacked up, huh? Who's your tip on that? June Cleaver?

MEDINA: Dating. Whatever.

ASHA: I'm not a lost and found.

MEDINA: Her name is Maya Ruiz.

Pause. ASHA is affected by the concern with which MEDINA speaks MAYA's name.

ASHA: I know.

MEDINA: You know?

ASHA: Paul Kelly is looking for her too.

MEDINA: Kelly? Why?

ASHA: He was hired by my client—

MEDINA: Who's your client?

ASHA: Grant Langdon. He wants me to deprogram his son, Matt Langdon, who is currently being held by police on suspicion in the possible homicide of his girlfriend, Maya Ruiz.

MEDINA looks stricken.

MEDINA: What evidence do they have?

ASHA: I was hoping maybe you could help me out with that.

MEDINA: You don't know?

ASHA: No. I was only just looped in. The dad doesn't seem to know much. Then again, his kid won't talk to him. But if they've hired Kelly to find the girl, then they don't have a body.

MEDINA suddenly seems extremely weary. He places both palms on ASHA's counter and drops his head. ASHA steps closer. She touches him.

ASHA: Reuben, I'm sorry.

MEDINA: Is that why you invited me in? You're sorry?

Jesus, Asha. What the fuck?

Would you have called me tonight? This connection—would you have told me if I hadn't just shown up here?

ASHA: I'm telling you now.

MEDINA: Bullshit, *now* you're *working a source.*

She doesn't deny it.

ASHA: Isn't that what *you're* doing?

Silence.

MEDINA exhales.

MEDINA: She called me.

ASHA stills.

Late at night. A couple weeks ago. I missed it. No voicemail, just—

I tried her back the next day. Her phone was turned off. Gave me a bad feeling, which I ignored. Kept trying her back. A few days later a neighbour reported her missing. Police couldn't do much with it. Finally, four days ago someone calls in her car in a ditch a few hours south of the city. That's enough that uniforms decide to pull her phone records. That's when they contact me—I'm her last outgoing call. They won't give me much, like I said, I've tried every in I have and nobody's talking. I finally got something yesterday from a clerk in the Flintland District—homicide unit applied for a warrant for the phone records of the boyfriend, Langdon. Served it just before taking him into holding this afternoon.

Silence.

It's eating me up. I keep thinking, if I'd picked up the phone—

ASHA: Reuben. This isn't on you.

MEDINA: They put their trust in me.

ASHA: Ruiz had moved out of Gamma House how long before this went down?

MEDINA: A couple years. I know she's not formally my responsibility, but—

ASHA: She's one of your kids. She'll always be one of your kids. I get it.

I really am sorry.

You're a good man, Medina. Maya Ruiz knew that. She knew you would have been there for her if you could.

Silence.

MEDINA: You think he killed her?

MEDINA seems lost.

ASHA: What do you think?

MEDINA: Answer something for me . . .

ASHA sighs.

ASHA: You want to know why I took Langdon's case.

MEDINA: You think it's an angle—a way to get at Holland.

His perceptiveness catches ASHA off guard.

ASHA: You sure that's it?

MEDINA: No. I honestly never know what you're thinking. But this Langdon thing reeks. I know you wouldn't normally get within a hundred feet of it—certainly not as a contractor for the defence.

ASHA: Maybe I want a nicer apartment.

MEDINA: Asha, there's nothing I'd believe you wanting enough to protect some dirtbag trust fund kid from charges for a crime he probably committed.

It's an inside track. Ammunition. Tell me I'm wrong.

ASHA: You've got me all figured out.

She moves away from him.

MEDINA: I don't want to tell you how to run your business—

ASHA: But you're going to.

He stifles whatever he was going to say.

What?

MEDINA: These guys are dangerous.

ASHA: You got any proof of that? Anything that would hold up in a court of law?

MEDINA: What do think Langdon's going to do if he finds out you're setting up his kid? What about Holland? You're telling me you don't think that guy's capable of protecting his interests?

ASHA: I'll deal with it.

MEDINA: Jesus Christ.

Silence. A standoff.

ASHA: You want to know why I didn't return your calls?

MEDINA sighs. It's an apology.

She looks at him.

You sounded *hopeful*.

I knew I couldn't tell you what you wanted to hear.

Another standoff—softer.

MEDINA: What do you want, Asha?

The question sits in the room. It feels to be about more than the case.

ASHA: I'm going into the station first thing tomorrow morning to try and meet with Matt Langdon—if he'll see me. I could use another set of eyes and ears.

MEDINA: And someone who can help you talk your way through the front door of a cop shop?

ASHA: That too.

He looks at her. He wonders if he's once again somehow played right into her hand.

MEDINA: Okay.

ASHA: I'll meet you there—let's say ten.

He heads to the door.

Medina?

He turns around. She hesitates, seeming to think better of whatever she'd wanted to say.

Thanks for the beer.

MEDINA nods. He exits.

ASHA takes the final swig of her beer. She sets it down. She goes to the window to watch MEDINA leave. She walks back over to the kitchen counter. She opens the shopping bag she'd set down when she first arrived. She pulls out a blouse. She holds it up and looks at it. She drapes it over her arm, taking it with her to the bedroom. On the way, she turns off the living room light.

From the street outside, MEDINA watches the light in ASHA's apartment go out. He waits another moment before he turns up his collar and sets out into the wet night.

Simultaneously, KATE closes up the diner. She locks the door and zips up her oversized hooded sweatshirt. She is headed east, toward the subway station. MEDINA is headed west. They pass one another in the street. MEDINA takes no notice of KATE. KATE keeps walking—eyes down and hood up. MEDINA vanishes into the rainy city. KATE keeps moving—she walks along a lonely stretch of road beneath an overpass where a huge, luminous LED billboard is mounted. The following text blooms on the advertisement:

"The Life You Are Destined To Have Is Determined By The Person You Are Content To Remain"

The text fades and is replaced with:

"What Are You Capable Of?"

The Luminia logo ("Luminia: The Science of Human Potential") appears below the "What Are You Capable Of?" text.

KATE stops. She looks up at the words. She keeps walking.

SCENE FOUR

An interview room in a police station. Early morning. ASHA *is alone in the interview room waiting to meet with* MATT *Langdon. Her attire this morning is a radical departure from the night before. She wears the blouse and a fitted skirt in soft colours, perhaps her hair is in a low chignon. The effect is that she appears younger and primmer—giving the impression of a paralegal, or maybe a* TA, *or a guidance councillor starting her first job at a private school. There is a visitor's badge clipped to her collar.*

MEDINA *and* BEECHUM *watch from the other side of a two-way mirror.* ASHA *(and later* MATT*) can't hear them.* MEDINA *and* BEECHUM *watch* ASHA *standing in the interview room, calmly waiting for* MATT.

MEDINA: Thank you, for this.

BEECHUM *shrugs.*

BEECHUM: Worth a shot. We've got to cut the kid loose in—

She looks at her watch

Ten hours. Unless we can rattle him—get something new.

MEDINA: You take a run yet?

BEECHUM: Yep.

MEDINA: What's your read?

BEECHUM: He's smart. Keeps his cards close.

Silence.

MEDINA: You think he killed the girl?

BEECHUM looks at him.

BEECHUM: No body.

MEDINA: That's not what I asked.

BEECHUM: Come on, Medina. No body, no crime. Not as far as prosecution is concerned. You know that. *You* taught me that.

MEDINA glances at the folder BEECHUM is carrying under her arm.

MEDINA: Are those the forensics on the car?

BEECHUM: Yeah.

MEDINA: Anything useful?

BEECHUM: You *know* I can't comment.

MEDINA: What are you holding him on?

BEECHUM: He's a person of interest.

MEDINA: Throw me a bone.

BEECHUM deliberates how much to tell him.

BEECHUM: We've got a phone message left by Maya Ruiz for Langdon the night we believe she went missing. Just before she called you. We had tech recover it when we subpoenaed the phone. Ruiz was distressed—her apartment had been broken into—

MEDINA: Broken into?

BEECHUM: Door kicked in, stuff tossed around—

MEDINA takes this in. He says nothing.

Anyway, she calls the boyfriend, distraught. She says she thinks she's in real danger.

MEDINA: And?

BEECHUM shrugs.

BEECHUM: Langdon deleted the message. Claimed he thought it was a prank or a cry for attention. Says Maya Ruiz is unstable and erratic. Not to mention a promiscuous drug user prone to disappear without notice for days on end.

She's looking at MEDINA, as if inviting him to contradict this.

She's got a sheet, which more or less backs his story: Possession, larceny. All a few years old—

MEDINA: Yeah. She cleaned up.

BEECHUM looks at him.

BEECHUM: You interact with her at all recently?

MEDINA: No.

BEECHUM notes something down.

So, that's it? A few old priors on *her*, and the little prick walks?

BEECHUM: It gives his account defensibility.

MEDINA: And Ruiz is just . . . disposable?

BEECHUM stares at him.

BEECHUM: Obviously not, but you can see how this is going to play.

Pause. MEDINA's jaw tightens.

MEDINA: Charge him on ignoring the voicemail.

BEECHUM: With what?

MEDINA: Negligence. Failing to take action to prevent grievous bodily harm—possibly death.

BEECHUM: We'd have to prove grievous bodily harm or death occurred.

For the moment, we're trying push for evidence tampering—deleting the message—withholding information in a missing persons investigation, but he knows it's thin.

The door to the interview room opens, MATT is brought in by two uniformed officers.

ASHA: Matt Langdon?

MATT: Yeah.

ASHA: I'm Asha. Nice to meet you.

ASHA lets MATT size her up.

How are you doing? You sleep all right?

He smiles. It's a self-assured smile, confident. In a different circumstance it would be charming. He takes a seat. She mirrors him, sitting opposite.

MATT: Sure.

ASHA: I can understand you're probably worried.

MATT: Not really.

He continues to look her over, with deep interest.

You a shrink or something?

ASHA: No.

MATT: Yeah, right.

He continues to regard her intently.

ASHA: I'm just a friend.

MATT: A friend, huh?

ASHA: I'm here to support you. I work with victims of trauma.

MATT looks bemused. Satisfied. He leans back in his chair.

MATT: So, a shrink.

ASHA says nothing.

My old man footing the bill for this?

ASHA: Your family is concerned about you.

MATT: Right.

ASHA: You don't believe that?

MATT folds his hands on the table. ASHA subtly mirrors the gesture.

MATT: So, what's the play here, Ashley?

ASHA doesn't correct him.

ASHA: I'm sorry?

MATT: I'm going to level with you . . .

He grins again, leaning in.

This Psych 101 stuff? You're killing it. Building a rapport, setting me at ease? Great work. Ten out of ten would confide all my problems to you. Here's the thing: you're wasting your time. I don't need a therapist. I don't need a lawyer. I sure as shit don't need a friend.

He sits back, looking at her.

But, hey, I wouldn't mind some attractive company and I know a girl's gotta eat, so here's what we'll do: you ask me all the thoughtful questions you're going to pretend like you haven't come prepared to hit me with, I'll respond with a bunch of hot nonsense, you can write down whatever you like, take that back to whoever you're not officially reporting to, and keep the cheque. Go buy yourself something nice.

He smiles. ASHA holds his gaze.

On the other side of the glass:

BEECHUM: Who is she again?

MEDINA: Deprogrammer. Like I said.

BEECHUM: Not really what I meant.

MEDINA: Don't bust my balls. She's a friend.

BEECHUM: You think she'll get anything?

MEDINA shrugs.

MEDINA: She's pretty good.

BEECHUM looks at him, her skepticism evident.

BEECHUM: Yeah?

MEDINA's expression doesn't give much away. He looks back through the glass.

ASHA: You want to talk about Maya Ruiz?

MATT: Not particularly.

ASHA: Why's that?

MATT: Pretty pissed at her right about now. I'm sure you can imagine.

I tell you what, when I get out of here *(putting on his best Ricky Ricardo impression)* she's gonna have some splainin' to do!

ASHA says nothing.

That was a joke, doc.

ASHA: She your girlfriend?

MATT: Nah. Maya doesn't like to label things. Not big on commitment, that one.

ASHA: What about you? You big on commitment?

MATT: Why, you looking for something serious?

ASHA: How long have you and Maya been dating?

MATT: We've been *hanging out* a few months. You know, off and on.

ASHA: Off and on?

MATT: When she's around.

ASHA: Where does she go? When she's not around?

MATT: No idea.

ASHA: You don't ask?

MATT leans in close again.

MATT: Between you and me, doc? Maya mixes with a lot of unsavoury people. Does some unsavoury things. Now, I'm not one to judge. Sometimes you just gotta cut loose, do a few lines, fuck some gangbangers, I get it. But I've got a future to think about, gotta keep my nose clean—I'd rather not know about any of that shit.

ASHA: Does it bother you?

MATT: Not at all. I support Maya in reaching the absolute fullest expression of herself. Hashtag "I'm with her."

Pause.

ASHA: That's a very progressive perspective

MATT: Hey, that's the world we live in now, right? Gotta make all kinds of concessions.

ASHA: Concessions?

MATT: Yeah, you know. Gotta be politically correct. Can't question the way anyone lives their life—might be offensive. Wouldn't want to be thought of as some old-school misogynistic prick with a limited world view trying to keep his bitch on a leash.

ASHA: Are you?

Pause. He looks at her.

Some misogynistic prick with a limited world view trying to keep his bitch on a leash?

Silence. Slowly, MATT *smiles.*

MATT: I'm sorry, Ashley. Did you find that offensive?

Silence.

Look, I'm going to give you some free advice. That kind of shit—it's only *offensive* if you let it offend you. If it *bothers* you, it's because of the meaning *you* are giving it. I just said some words. *You* are the one internalizing them and giving them power to upset you. Being *upset* or *offended* is just a loss of control—a temper tantrum—its projecting your own unresolved shit on another person for just saying *words*.

The problem is that not enough people are willing to work on themselves—correct what needs to be corrected in their own thinking, so that they're capable of existing in this world without being fucking *triggered* by every interaction with another person. Expecting me to police everything coming out of my mouth instead of taking any responsibility for the "offence" you are choosing to feel in reaction to it is ridiculous.

You want to be empowered? Stop letting agenda-pushing leftist media tell you how to think—tell you what you should react to. Stop reading *Teen Vogue* articles that tell you that you are a victim. There's no such thing as a victim—only a person too stunted to figure out how to evolve beyond taking every fucking thing personally.

The way you experience your life is a choice. You *choose* to wake up every day and carry that shit around with you. Just think: what could you do with all that capacity, if you weren't lugging all of that around all the time? If you weren't constantly managing your self-imposed *trauma*, what would you be capable of?

ASHA's expression gives nothing away.

ASHA: Did Maya want to put in the work?

MATT: Maya is a creature of the moment.

ASHA: She was going to leave Luminia?

MATT regards her with suspicion.

MATT: I don't know. You'll have to ask her when she turns up.

ASHA: Would that bother you?

MATT: No, it wouldn't. As I have made very clear, she can do whatever she wants.

ASHA looks at him intently.

ASHA: You know her pretty well.

MATT: I guess.

ASHA: So, what do you think happened?

MATT looks straight at ASHA.

MATT: I don't think anything happened.

He leans in.

My theory, if you're interested, is that Maya's just fine. My *theory* is that she's found some dumb cuck who's richer and easier to manipulate, and right now she's out there somewhere blowing him for Sephora money and getting off thinking about ruining my fucking day.

ASHA: You seem angry, Matt.
Are you sure I can't provide you with some tools to help you process this?

She opens her hands, palms up, on the table. MATT blinks at her. Something in what she's said combined with this gesture has suddenly made him very uneasy.

MATT: I don't need tools.

ASHA: A suggestion, then:

Be careful about doling out "free advice" derived from course materials that aren't your intellectual property and aren't to be spoken about publicly.

MATT says nothing, but his fear is evident.

MATT: Who are you?

ASHA: Like I said. I'm a friend. *Your family is concerned about you.*

For the first time since his arrival, MATT *appears very concerned.*

Matt, I've got a theory too, about Maya Ruiz. If you're interested.

MATT: Oh yeah?

He shifts in his seat. Trying to seem nonchalant.

ASHA: I think that you do care what she does.

I think when you came by her apartment and she wasn't there you got pissed.

I think you kicked in her door.

MATT: What?

ASHA: I think you tossed her stuff. Then, I think you hid and waited for her to come home. When she did, I think you fought about where she'd been.

For the first time since entering the room, MATT *looks toward the mirror.*

MATT: This is bullshit—

ASHA: I think you strangled her—

MATT *scoffs.* ASHA *continues, nonplussed.*

I think you strangled her . . . on the floor between the couch and the coffee table. Then I think you wrapped her in the blue throw from off the armchair and dumped her in the tub.

MATT has gone completely stony.

Then, I think you called Richard Holland.

MATT looks up at her.

I believe you confessed what you'd done and pleaded for his help. At which point, Mr. Holland advised you to call the police and confess your crime.

MATT is gaping at her.

Disregarding his counsel, I believe you packed Maya Ruiz into the trunk of her vehicle and drove out to Salter Wildlife Park, where you disposed of her remains in a culvert four miles southeast of the water maintenance facility. I believe you then drove the vehicle another hour south, abandoning it near a truck stop with a reputation for drug activity, in order to mislead investigators.

ASHA stands. MATT is paralyzed.

As you know, integrity and honesty are core tenants of Luminia's values doctrine.

She touches his shoulder.

Mr. Holland knows you'll do the right thing.

ASHA exits the interview room. She enters the space behind the mirror from which MEDINA and BEECHUM have been watching. They both stare at her with incredulity.

MEDINA: What the *hell* was that?

BEECHUM is suddenly on her radio.

BEECHUM: *(into the radio)* Ballard, what's your twenty?

ASHA: *(still looking into the interview room through the glass)* There. He's going to ask for a lawyer. He thinks Holland is selling him out.

Something garbled comes back from Sgt. Ballard over the radio.

BEECHUM: *(to ASHA)* I need your source.

ASHA: I don't have one.

BEECHUM regards her with extreme skepticism.

BEECHUM: You don't have one?

ASHA: That's correct.

BEECHUM looks from ASHA to MEDINA.

BEECHUM sighs.

BEECHUM: *(into the radio, while eyeing ASHA and MEDINA)* Ballard, yeah, I need an available unit to run down an anonymous tip. A possible 10-54 in Salter Wildlife Park—southeast of the water treatment facility.

BEECHUM leaves the room. ASHA and MEDINA follow.

SCENE FIVE (A)

ASHA and MEDINA descend the stairs outside the police station. ASHA walks purposefully—she's in a hurry. MEDINA chases after her.

MEDINA: Asha—

He speeds up.

ASHA! Damn it. STOP.

MEDINA grabs her arm. She stops. She turns around. He sees that she's distressed. It's maybe the first time he's seen her upset. He softens whatever he was going to say.

What's going on?

ASHA: Leave it.

MEDINA: Like hell.

Silence.

What are they going to find? Beechum and her people—what are they going to find in Salter Park?

Silence. She looks away.

Goddamn it. Give me *something*.

ASHA: I can't, Reuben. Not yet.

He tries to process this. She starts walking again.

MEDINA: Where are you going?

ASHA: I've got something I've got to do.

MEDINA: Where?

ASHA: Capitol Point.

Pause.

MEDINA: *What?*

ASHA: Back off, Medina.

MEDINA: Are you taking a run at Holland?

ASHA: No.

MEDINA: I'm coming.

ASHA: You're not invited.

MEDINA: It's a public campus.

She stops. She stares at him.

ASHA: Don't even think about it.

She starts walking again.

MEDINA: Have you seen his sheet?

ASHA: No.

MEDINA: The guy is—

ASHA: Dangerous. I'm aware.

MEDINA: I was going to say: careful.

ASHA: I'm aware of that, too. What's on the sheet?

MEDINA: Nothing.

ASHA stops at this.

ASHA: Are you serious?

MEDINA: Yeah.

She closes her eyes and exhales.

Is that surprising?

ASHA: It's disappointing.

ASHA starts walking again.

MEDINA: Who is this guy?

They turn a corner. ASHA stops at a twenty-four-hour hot dog cart, Franco's Franks. She takes a napkin from its holder and quickly writes something on it. She folds it up. She pulls out two twenties from her wallet and passes them both, alongside the folded-up napkin, to FRANCO.

ASHA: *(to FRANCO)* Hey, I've got friend who will be coming buy about 8 p.m. Think you can give him that?

FRANCO stares at the folded napkin, and then at the forty dollars. He nods. He takes the napkin and the bills.

Thank you.

FRANCO passes her a hot dog.

FRANCO: Best dogs west of West 76th!

She takes it. She looks at MEDINA.

ASHA: *(to MEDINA)* Best dogs west of West 76th. You want one?

He shakes his head, his bewilderment evident. ASHA starts walking again, eating her hot dog. MEDINA looks back over his shoulder to Franco's Franks, then back to ASHA.

MEDINA: What was that?

ASHA: Analog voicemail.

MEDINA: Unbelievable.

Silence as ASHA keeps walking and eating her hot dog.

Hey, Watergate. Wait up. I'm trying to talk to you.

ASHA: Listen, you need to leave this alone.

MEDINA: Not going to happen.

ASHA: I'm telling you—

MEDINA: Telling me what? Doesn't feel like you're telling me anything.

ASHA: What should I be telling you?

MEDINA: How about telling me how you seem to have intimate knowledge of a violent homicide?

ASHA: Just don't get near this thing, okay? Just walk away.

MEDINA: Why?

ASHA: Because Maya Ruiz would want you to.

It's a low blow, and they both know it.

MEDINA: That's not fair.

ASHA: I know.

Pause.

MEDINA: You'll have to testify. If they find her in the park.

ASHA: I know.

MEDINA: You okay with that?

Pause.

ASHA: She's not in the park.

Pause.

MEDINA: You *moved* remains?

ASHA: Of course not.

MEDINA: I don't understand.

ASHA: Good. Don't. Don't understand. Drop it altogether.

MEDINA: Not going to happen.

Something occurs to MEDINA.

How are you getting to Capital Point?

ASHA: I'm taking the M Train, but—

MEDINA: Okay. I've got a quick errand to run, and then I'll meet you up there.

ASHA: You've—what?

MEDINA: Half an hour. Give me half an hour.

MEDINA *starts to jog back toward the police station.*

ASHA: I'm not waiting for you! Medina—!

He's gone. ASHA *keeps walking quickly toward the train station.*

MEDINA *runs back past Franco's Franks. He stops suddenly. Inspiration has struck. He doubles back.*

MEDINA: *(to* FRANCO*)* Hi there, sir. Listen, I'm wondering if you would be willing to accept *(digging bills from his wallet)* . . . a hundred dollars . . . for that napkin my friend just gave you? And a couple dozen dogs?

FRANCO *looks at the bills. He nods. He hands* MEDINA *the note and begins to package up his dogs.*

FRANCO: Best dogs west of / West 76th!

MEDINA: / West 76th, I know.

MEDINA opens up ASHA's note. He reads it. He frowns. He pockets it.

SCENE FIVE (B)

Simultaneously, the following:

BEECHUM leads a team of uniformed officers as they search Salter Park.

MEDINA takes the hot dogs back to the police station bullpen, where he starts handing them out. In the process, he casually sneaks a look at the distinctive folder with the forensic findings on MAYA's vehicle that BEECHUM has left on her desk.

ASHA arrives at the Luminia Campus in Capitol Point. It looks more like a medium-budget television studio than an educational facility. Monitors are everywhere depicting multiple angles of what appears to be a man (HOLLAND) giving a motivational lecture to an eager studio audience. ASHA carries a Dairy Queen box containing an ice cream cake. She approaches the reception desk, indicating to the harried-looking receptionist that she's dropping off the cake. The receptionist holds up a finger to indicate "give me one minute, I'm on the phone." ASHA shrugs and sets the cake down on top of the paperwork on the desk, then "leaves," moving out of sight of the desk. The receptionist picks up the cake—which is beginning to melt—and looks around helplessly for someone to take it. With nobody immediately around, she makes the decision to temporarily abandon her post to take the melting cake to a freezer, presumably located in some interior office. ASHA takes advantage of her absence to surreptitiously unplug a couple things from the desk's computer at random, and then plug them back in incorrectly. ASHA *slips out of sight again. The receptionist returns and takes her seat. She clicks the computer's mouse and frowns. She tries a couple things to rectify the problem, to no avail. She picks up the phone and dials an extension.*

SCENE SIX

ASHA waits in the Luminia Campus lobby, just out of sight of the main reception desk. She watches the comings and goings of people around her, seeming to be texting, or possible really texting. MEDINA arrives. He approaches her—surprised to find her waiting.

MEDINA: Didn't think you'd be waiting for me.

ASHA: I'm not.

He realizes she's watching the reception desk, where the receptionist and another staffer—an IT technician—are preoccupied with the computer.

MEDINA: What's going on?

ASHA: She's having IT issues.

MEDINA stares at ASHA, fully aware she has something to do with this.

The technical issue now appears to be resolved, and the technician leaves, squeezing past ASHA, who has suddenly become engrossed in her phone and seems unaware she's obstructing his exit path. He disappears somewhere deeper into the building.

(to MEDINA) Come on.

MEDINA follows ASHA across the lobby to another, more important looking door. ASHA looks back over to the reception desk—the receptionist is occupied. ASHA produces a key card and taps it against the sensor. The door unlocks. MEDINA glares at her as he follows her through.

MEDINA: Where did you get that?

ASHA: IT technicians have the most extensive building security permissions.

MEDINA: You *picked* his *pocket*?

MEDINA clenches his jaw. He's supremely uncomfortable with this.

ASHA: What?

MEDINA: Nothing.

They move through the hallway with purpose. ASHA clearly has a destination in mind.

I thought you were meeting with Holland.

ASHA: Holland's not here.

MEDINA: Where is he?

ASHA indicates the omnipresent monitors showing different angles of the man on the stage giving the motivational lecture.

ASHA: Down on the sound stage. He's been speaking all morning.

MEDINA: Is that on television. Who sees that?

ASHA: It's a livestream. Anyone with a Wi-Fi connection.

MEDINA: Speaking about what?

ASHA: Individual exceptionalism.

MEDINA: What?

ASHA: "Why You Matter More Than Other People 101."

MEDINA: People really go for this?

ASHA: Some people.

MEDINA: Why?

ASHA sighs.

ASHA: It's complicated. Medina, nobody wakes up one day and thinks: today I'm going to join a cult.

MEDINA: Asha—

He stops moving abruptly, noticing the surveillance cameras.

There are cameras all over this place.

ASHA: Yeah, I know. Keep moving and try not to stare straight into them.

MEDINA: We're breaking the law here.

ASHA: And you can leave at any time, narc.

She reaches her destination. They stop, faced with another closed door.

ASHA: Okay. Let's try this.

MEDINA: Where are we?

ASHA: Holland's office. I hope.

She taps the key card against the sensor. The door unlocks. They enter the room—she's correct, it's HOLLAND*'s office. They stand in the space.* ASHA *has gone stiff and quiet—she is caught off guard by the effect* HOLLAND*'s space has on her.* MEDINA *looks around. It's a normal executive office. There's a television monitor with the same feed as elsewhere, but no security cameras.*

MEDINA: No cameras in this room.

ASHA: *(softly)* Nope.

He looks at ASHA.

MEDINA: Are you all right?

ASHA *nods. She exhales. She starts to go through* HOLLAND*'s things, not taking particularly great care to put things back exactly as she found them.*

What are you looking for?

ASHA: I'm not.

MEDINA: Then what are you doing?

She thinks about how to explain.

ASHA: I want him rattled.

MEDINA: Why?

ASHA: I *know* guys like this—

MEDINA: You know guys like this, or you know Holland specifically?

ASHA looks at him. She doesn't answer.

ASHA: He needs to feel in control. Take that away from him—violate his space—and he'll lose it. It might give your cop friends a better shot at getting something useful when they bring him in—

MEDINA: Do you think that's what they're going to do?

ASHA: Wouldn't you?

MEDINA: Depends what Matt Langdon does.

ASHA: What do you mean?

MEDINA: You put Langdon's high-price lawyers back in the picture. Maybe they advise him to just keep his mouth shut. Honestly, Asha, any decent legal counsel will shut down a deal. Unless he's *absolutely certain* damning evidence is about to come to light, they'll keep him quiet.

ASHA: He's certain.

MEDINA: How do you know?

ASHA: Because, I was looking him in the eyes. He knows we know what he did. He believes that the police unit out there combing the woods right now is going to find where he dumped her. He's panicking. If he's told those lawyers that, they're going to look for anything Langdon can offer in exchange for reduced charges.

MEDINA: And what do you think he's got?

ASHA: Holland is involved in this. I'm sure.

MEDINA: How?

ASHA: I don't know.

MEDINA: Then how are you so sure he's involved?

Silence. ASHA opens HOLLAND's desk drawer. She sweeps its contents around.

ASHA: It's his MO.

MEDINA: What's his MO?

ASHA: Stuff the girl's body in a storm drain in the woods.

MEDINA stares at her.

MEDINA: Holland has a clean rap sheet.

ASHA: I understand that. I'm *telling you* it's his MO.

ASHA shuts the desk drawer. MEDINA just watches her. He looks up at the TV monitor of the sound stage.

MEDINA: Uh-oh.

ASHA: What?

MEDINA: *Shit.*

ASHA: What?

MEDINA: We've got company.

He points. Uniformed officers have arrived and are on the sound stage speaking with HOLLAND.

SCENE SEVEN (A)

The police station. BEECHUM *and* ROMERO *regard* HOLLAND *through the two-way mirror.* HOLLAND *appears nonplussed about the situation. He waits patiently.*

Behind the glass:

ROMERO: So, I hear the park was a bust.

BEECHUM*'s expression is carefully blank.*

BEECHUM: So far.

ROMERO: Tough break.

BEECHUM: We got a signed confession from the kid, right?

ROMERO: Yeah. He's copping to the death—though he's calling it an accident—and he's offered up your guy Holland here on accessory-after-the-fact. But it's gonna be hard to make that stick.

BEECHUM: Why?

ROMERO: No corroboration. A "he said, he said."

They both look through the glass at HOLLAND.

BEECHUM: What are the specifics?

ROMERO: Langdon is now claiming coercion, essentially. He admits to the fight with the girlfriend—says things "got out of hand" and the next thing he knew Ruiz was dead.

ROMERO and BEECHUM exchange a look.

That's where it gets interesting though. Langdon does admit to calling Holland after her death but refutes the nature of the conversation described by your consultant. He's claiming that he called his "spiritual advisor" to confess what he'd done and stated that—prior to the call—it had been his intention to notify law enforcement.

It's Langdon's testimony that Holland "became enraged" and "threatened him," as he believed Langdon's admission of the crime would be damaging to the public image of Luminia.

Langdon says Holland forbade him from coming forward and devised the plan to dispose of Maya Ruiz's remains, which Langdon admits to executing—

BEECHUM: Hold on. Langdon *admits* to dumping the body of Maya Ruiz in Salter Wildlife Park?

ROMERO: Yeah.

BEECHUM: In a culvert southeast of the water treatment plant?

ROMERO: Yeah.

Pause.

Maybe someone moved it? Maybe Holland—

BEECHUM: According to Langdon, Holland was the one who told him to dump her there.

ROMERO: Well, maybe Langdon didn't actually follow through?

BEECHUM: That kid was terrified when the site was first mentioned. It's what motivated him to lawyer up and look for a deal. If he'd taken her somewhere different, he'd have been relieved we were going out to look in the wrong place.

ROMERO: What if Holland moved Ruiz after the fact?

BEECHUM: I mean . . . I guess it's possible.

She stares back through the glass.

ROMERO: Donovan knows him.

BEECHUM looks at her.

BEECHUM: The kid?

ROMERO: The professor.

BEECHUM: How?

ROMERO: I think they golf together.

Pause.

He doesn't like that you brought him in. Doesn't think it was necessary.

BEECHUM: Good thing it's not his case.

Pause.

ROMERO: You think that's smart?

BEECHUM: What?

ROMERO: I don't know. Riling Donovan.

BEECHUM: I'm doing my job.

Pause.

ROMERO: He's been tipped for captain. After Darby retires.

BEECHUM: I know.

ROMERO: Might be smart to tread lightly, there.

Pause.

BEECHUM: You want to say something to me?

ROMERO: Reuben Medina.

BEECHUM: What about him?

ROMERO: You liked working under him?

BEECHUM: Medina was solid.

ROMERO: That's what I heard. I heard he was exceptional.

BEECHUM: And?

ROMERO: And he's not on the job anymore. Because he was a pain in the ass. Picked the wrong fights. Didn't know when to back down. Couldn't make nice.

Pause.

I like working with you.

Pause.

BEECHUM: I'm not going anywhere.

ROMERO: You might not have a choice.

Pause.

BEECHUM: What else do we have on Holland?

ROMERO opens up a file. It's thin.

ROMERO: Nothing criminal. A couple of minor harassment complaints that didn't get too far.

BEECHUM: Why not?

ROMERO: Hard to say. Looks like there wasn't much to them. No minors. No blood.

BEECHUM: What were they?

ROMERO looks at the pages in the folder.

ROMERO: There's a complaint here from a former assistant who says Holland would summon her to his hotel room to take dictation for him in phone meetings while he walked around in the nude.

A few groping incidents—the most notable of which occurred during a live broadcast. He put his hand up an audience member's skirt.

She looks at BEECHUM.

Apparently, he was illustrating a point about determinism.

BEECHUM: Great.

They both look back through the glass. BEECHUM *takes the folder from* ROMERO *and enters the interview room.* ROMERO *watches from the other side of the glass.*

Mr. Holland.

She approaches him and shakes his hand. She takes her seat.

I'm Detective Alison Beechum. Thank you for coming in and meeting with us.

HOLLAND *nods. His expression seems tired, downcast.*

HOLLAND: It's an awful thing.

BEECHUM *observes him.*

BEECHUM: How do you know Matthew Langdon?

HOLLAND: Matt is part of our Luminia family.

BEECHUM: Can you elaborate on that?

HOLLAND: Luminia is a community of like-minded individuals committed to self-improvement. Matt was one of us.

BEECHUM: How long has Matt been part of your . . . group.

HOLLAND: Almost three years, I believe.

BEECHUM: How would you describe your relationship?

HOLLAND: I mentored Matt closely.

BEECHUM: Sorry—you said that Matt Langdon "was" one of you? Does this mean his current status is in jeopardy?

HOLLAND thinks about this.

HOLLAND: Luminia holds some core tenets around the expected behaviour of its membership. Moreover, Matt's actions these past weeks—as I understand them—are deeply disturbing to me. At this point, Ms. Beechum, I don't believe I could continue our relationship.

BEECHUM: Detective.

He meets her gaze.

HOLLAND: Detective.

BEECHUM: Was Maya Ruiz also a member of the Luminia family?

HOLLAND: I didn't know Ms. Ruiz personally, but I believe she participated in some of our programming—

BEECHUM: What sort of programming?

HOLLAND: It's my understanding that Ms. Ruiz was recovering from an addiction.

BEECHUM: Is that a support service you offer?

HOLLAND: We always recommend individuals seek appropriate therapies through licensed practitioners, but Luminia offers ongoing outpatient treatments, as well as motivational seminars and leadership training.

BEECHUM: I understand that Maya Ruiz and Matthew Langdon were involved, is that correct?

HOLLAND: That is what I now understand, yes.

BEECHUM: Are your members allowed to become involved?

HOLLAND: Ms. Beechum—

BEECHUM: Detective

Almost imperceptibly, HOLLAND *clenches his jaw.*

HOLLAND: Detective. Luminia is not a prison, nor a monastery. We encourage our membership to live rich and fulfilling lives.

Pause.

BEECHUM: Matt Langdon called you after his altercation with Ms. Ruiz, is that correct?

HOLLAND: Yes.

BEECHUM: Do you recall what you discussed?

HOLLAND *sighs. He hangs his head—a portrait of deep sadness.*

HOLLAND: Matthew was distraught. He was rambling. His speech was incoherent. I struggled to understand him. After several minutes, he revealed to me that he was at Ms. Ruiz's apartment, that there had been an altercation.

BEECHUM: Did he provide you with any details of what had occurred, at that time?

HOLLAND: No. He was ranting about . . . he wasn't in a sound headspace.

BEECHUM: Ranting about . . . ?

HOLLAND: Harlots. About Jezebel and Delilah. Betrayal. About sin and damnation.

BEECHUM: Are these themes you'd discussed previously?

HOLLAND: No. Luminia discourages the integration of pervasive cultural mythologies in our teachings.

BEECHUM: You quote Ayn Rand.

HOLLAND blinks at her.

Often, actually. You quote her in a lot of your materials, but you don't credit her.

HOLLAND: I don't understand your accusation.

BEECHUM: Just an observation.

Pause.

Did you believe Matthew Langdon was in danger, when you spoke with him?

HOLLAND: No.

BEECHUM: Did you believe Maya Ruiz was in danger?

Silence.

HOLLAND: I didn't want to believe Matt was capable of . . . what he had described.

BEECHUM: What did he describe?

HOLLAND: He said he'd killed her.

BEECHUM: Did you believe him?

Silence.

HOLLAND: Yes.

BEECHUM: What action did you take then?

HOLLAND looks down again, seemingly contrite.

HOLLAND: I told him—
I said that this was a testing moment
That he had an obligation now, to his community, to his family
To do the right thing.

BEECHUM: What was Mr. Langdon's response

HOLLAND: He concurred.

Pause.

BEECHUM: Mr. Holland, did you make any effort, yourself, to notify the proper authorities about the crime that had been disclosed to you?

HOLLAND: No.

BEECHUM: Why not?

HOLLAND: Because I believed that taking ownership of the offence was necessary for Matthew—on his journey. I believed that it would be essential to his rehabilitation.

BEECHUM nods.

BEECHUM: Mr. Holland, have you ever been to Ms. Ruiz's apartment?

HOLLAND: No.

BEECHUM: How about Salter Wildlife Park?

HOLLAND: No.

BEECHUM: How about the Rock Ridge Truck Stop off Highway 6?

Something flickers in HOLLAND's expression.

HOLLAND: Not to my recollection.

BEECHUM regards him intently.

BEECHUM: Do you have anything else you'd like to add?

HOLLAND: Not at this time.

BEECHUM nods. She stands.

BEECHUM: Thank you for your time.

She exits the interview room, entering the other space where ROMERO still waits.

ROMERO: Langdon's lawyers are going to jump all over that "do the right thing" bit.

BEECHUM: Yeah. I know.

ROMERO: What do you think?

BEECHUM: I think the truck stop bothered him.

ROMERO: Is that enough?

BEECHUM: To hold him? No.

ROMERO: So, what do you want to do?

BEECHUM: Cut him loose.

BEECHUM stares back through the glass.

And turn his life inside out.

She exits.

SCENE SEVEN (B)

The Clairmont. KATE shuts the place down for the night. She gives the counter a final wipe. She turns off the kitchen lights and locks the till. She grabs her backpack and her jacket from somewhere in back. She takes one last look around to make sure she's completed all her the closing duties. She digs an envelope out of her apron pocket and places it on the counter. She takes the name badge off her uniform and sets it on top of the envelope. She takes one last look around before she leaves the diner, locking the door behind her.

SCENE EIGHT (A)

MEDINA stakes out Franco's Franks. It's almost 8 p.m. It's started to rain again, and darkness is setting in. MEDINA watches as Paul KELLY approaches the hot dog cart. MEDINA intercepts him.

MEDINA: Hey Paul. You got a minute?

KELLY: Reuben Medina? Is that you?

MEDINA: Yeah, it's me. Good to see you, man.

KELLY: Almost didn't recognize you out uniform.

MEDINA: Haven't worn the uniform in a lot of years.

KELLY: Yeah, I know. It's a shame, that. You were one hell of a cop. Never understood why you gave it up.

MEDINA shrugs, trying for a casualness he doesn't feel.

MEDINA: Badge started to wear me.

KELLY regards him thoughtfully.

I don't know. I guess . . .

He finds the most truthful explanation he can.

I just felt like there were better ways to help people.

KELLY: And the missus had had enough?

MEDINA: That too, I guess. 'Course that situation was pretty far gone by then—I don't think leaving the job ended up making too much of a difference there, in the end.

KELLY: Sorry to hear that.

MEDINA: It is what it is.

Pause.

KELLY: What can I do for you, Reuben?

MEDINA: I've got a message for you—from Asha Ray.

MEDINA hands over the napkin.

KELLY: Oh yeah? You reading my mail?

KELLY opens the note and looks it.

MEDINA: What's she thanking you for?

KELLY looks at MEDINA, unsure if he should answer.

KELLY: Why don't you ask her?

MEDINA: Look, Kelly, I'm sorry. I don't want to put you in a tough spot, but I really need to understand this thing. It's heating up and I'm worried. I think she's in danger. I want to help, but she's freezing me out. I just want to know what's going on. What's the "thank you" about?

KELLY thinks about how much to reveal.

KELLY: I gave her the Langdon case.

MEDINA: You mean, you recommended her services to Grant Langdon?

KELLY: Yeah, like she asked.

MEDINA: She *asked you* to refer her to Grant Langdon?

KELLY: Yeah.

MEDINA: How did she know he was looking to hire a deprogrammer?

KELLY: He wasn't. He was trying to find a missing girl.

MEDINA: Maya Ruiz.

KELLY: Yeah.

I contacted Asha to ask her if she might know anything about where this girl might be. She said she didn't, but she wanted to be put on the case. She asked if maybe Langdon could use a deprogrammer.

I don't know—felt like maybe she had an axe to grind there. Maybe I shouldn't have gotten her involved, but I owe her a few favours . . .

This is surprising to MEDINA.

MEDINA: Why'd you contact Asha—at first—about the girl?

KELLY: I was hopeful.

MEDINA: Hopeful about what?

KELLY looks at MEDINA intently, realizing he really doesn't know.

KELLY: I've been a PI a lot of years, Reuben. And I've seen some things. A lot of truly heartbreaking shit out there. And mostly there's not a lot you can do for people, but you gotta try, right? Sometimes there are just those circumstances where you gotta try to do something. Buy someone a sandwich, or a jacket, or a SIM card, or bus ticket, you know? Except sometimes they need more than a bus ticket—you know what I'm saying?

Silence.

MEDINA: Not sure.

KELLY: What does Asha Ray *do*?

The question sits for a moment.

MEDINA: She . . . pulls people out of impossible situations. She brings them back—she finds them.

KELLY: She also hides them.

Silence.

Over the years I've come to her with a few cases: good people—generally women—in bad situations. Women who needed protecting from something—a john, or a dealer, or a shitbag husband. Women without a lot of legal recourse. Or resources. Asha's gotten them out, gotten them situated—

MEDINA: What, you mean like witness protection?

KELLY: Yeah. Without the paper trail. And sometimes behind the back of the law.

Silence.

MEDINA: You came to her about Maya Ruiz, because you thought—

KELLY: I hoped maybe she knew something that I didn't.

MEDINA: Did she?

KELLY: No.

KELLY sighs heavily.

I guess sometimes we're just too late.

KELLY tucks the napkin into his pocket. He claps MEDINA on the arm. He departs. MEDINA remains standing in the street, lost in thought. His phone rings, he picks it up.

MEDINA: Medina.

BEECHUM: Hey. I know you wanted to be kept in the loop on the Ruiz case—

MEDINA: What's up?

BEECHUM: We got a break.

MEDINA: What kind of break?

BEECHUM: Remains.

MEDINA is hit by a wave of deep sadness.

MEDINA: Where? In Salter Park?

BEECHUM: No. Nearby.
Holland was cagey this afternoon about having been to that truck stop.

We looked into it—

MEDINA: You got a warrant together already?

BEECHUM: No. Showed a picture of Holland to the owner—she recognized him. Says he's been a customer for years. His family used to have property nearby, but it was all converted into a wetland conservation area a while back, due south of Salter Park. We got a unit out there now and the K9s got a hit. Not much in the way of details. I'm heading out there now. Preliminary suggestions are good, though—remains are female, young, found in a runoff shunt.

Silence.

MEDINA: Thank you, Alison.

Silence.

BEECHUM: I'll let you know when I have more.

MEDINA: Drive safe.

MEDINA hangs up.

Darkness has fully settled. Billboards and neon signage flicker to life. The moon is high.

SCENE EIGHT (B)

A residential neighbourhood across town. KATE walks along the dappled sidewalk, moving in and out of the moonlit shadows of the giant oaks lining the street. The homes here are huge. The night is uncommonly quiet. KATE arrives at her destination— a large, sprawling Georgian mansion on a corner lot. She steps out of the shadows into the moon-washed driveway and stares up at the house. There are lights on in the main living areas downstairs, as well a single bedroom light glowing in one of the upstairs bedrooms. She stands in the drive a long moment, staring at the illuminated upstairs window. There is a noise—a dog barks, or a car door slams—and she is jolted back to reality. She steps back into the cover of the oak trees.

SCENE NINE

ASHA's apartment. Nighttime. She is boxing, aggressively punching the punching bag. The buzzer goes. She ignores it. It buzzes again. She goes over to the buzzer.

ASHA: What?

MEDINA: *(over the intercom)* It's me. Can I come up?

ASHA: No.

She goes back to the punching bag. He buzzes repeatedly until she eventually relents and lets him in. She pours herself a glass of water and drains most of it—she's been training hard. MEDINA *comes into the apartment.*

What do you want, Medina?

He takes in her state.

MEDINA: Are you okay?

ASHA: I'm fine.

She goes back to hitting the punching bag. He takes off his wet coat and drapes it over the counter. To MEDINA, ASHA *seems tightly wound—edgy—more volatile than usual.*

MEDINA: I thought you'd have wanted to stick around this afternoon—watch the interview with Holland.

ASHA: No.

MEDINA: Why not?

ASHA: Is he still in custody?

MEDINA: Not at the moment.

ASHA: That's why.

He debates telling her about the call he's just had with BEECHUM. He decides not to.

MEDINA: They'll be bringing him back in soon.

ASHA: Great. I can't wait.

MEDINA: Where'd you go? With your free afternoon?

ASHA: Nowhere. Bought a treat for myself. Came back here and tried not to crawl out of my own skin.

MEDINA: A treat, huh?

ASHA: New tape.

She shows him her taped-up fists.

MEDINA: Matt Langdon's going to testify that Richard Holland coerced him into concealing his crime and gave him instructions about disposing of the remains.

ASHA: Huh. And what's going to happen to Langdon?

MEDINA: Charges with mitigating circumstances.

ASHA: Mitigating circumstances, such as?

MEDINA: Being unduly influenced by Holland. Stress. His academic and athletic record.

ASHA: Where is he now?

MEDINA: Langdon? With his parents. He bailed out a couple hours ago.

ASHA: So, you're saying that both Richard Holland and Matt Langdon are currently just . . . at home? What, microwaving pizzas? Watching reruns of *The Voice*?

> *She begins to hit the punching bag with greater intensity.* MEDINA *braces it for her.*

I can't deal with that.

MEDINA: I know.

ASHA: *Jesus Christ.*

> *She hits the punching bag in silence for a few moments as* MEDINA *holds it.*

MEDINA: I'm sorry, Asha.

> *She continues to hit the bag. As she does, it's as though the actual reality of all this information—a lot of which she likely already knew or suspected—churns inside her and anger threatens to overwhelm her self-control.*

ASHA: I'm really, really tired, Medina.

MEDINA: I know.

ASHA: I'm tired of these men lying or threatening or buying or bullshitting their way out of consequence.

I'm tired of the suit in the court system who looked over Matt Langdon's file this afternoon and decided that his *athletics track record* should factor into a mitigating circumstances plea.

I'm tired of these entitled predators walking around in the world knowing they can't be touched—*knowing* there will always be a deal on the table for them.

Matt Langdon will *be* Richard Holland in twenty years. And Richard Holland will keep being Richard Holland for the remainder of his natural life and how many people do you think they'll brutalize along the way?

I can't deal with that.

> *ASHA trails off. She's stopped hitting the punching bag. She wipes her eyes with the back of her forearm. She is breathing hard—extreme physical exertion and emotion have both caught up with her.*
>
> *MEDINA can't tell if she's crying.*
>
> *ASHA takes another swing at the punching bag—MEDINA intercedes. The momentum of ASHA's swing carries her into him. He tucks her head against his chest and holds her to him—it's a gesture of deep understanding and empathy. He feels helpless. They remain like this for a moment until ASHA's breathing steadies.*
>
> *She pulls back slightly, looking at him.*
>
> *ASHA kisses MEDINA. He responds, drawing her against him. The kiss deepens, becoming heated. MEDINA pulls back.*

MEDINA: We've got him on this, okay? I promise. Richard Holland is going to jail.

Asha, they found her.

She stares at him.

ASHA: What?

MEDINA: Maya. They found her remains. They were in a wetland conservation area, south of Salter Park. Alison felt like there was something wrong with Holland's denial of having been to the truck stop so they dug in—learned he's a regular with family ties to the area. They expanded the search. Alison called me on my way over here—they don't have any details yet, but the word is it's a young woman, found in a drainage culvert.

We've got him.

ASHA has turned absolutely rigid. She pulls away from MEDINA.

ASHA: He's going to flee.

MEDINA: He's not going to flee. Asha, look at me. They'll have him under surveillance until they're ready to make the arrest—probably in the next few hours.

ASHA: They're staking out his home?

MEDINA: Yeah.

ASHA picks up her keys from the kitchen counter. She digs something metal out of her purse.

Where are you going?

ASHA: Sorry about this.

MEDINA: Asha—

He reaches for her. In flash, she's got him in a grappling hold. Before he's worked out what's happening, she's handcuffed him to the radiator. He stares at her in utter disbelief as she pats him down.

ASHA: Where's your phone?

MEDINA: Are you fucking serious?
It's in my jacket—on the counter—it's—

ASHA: Good. Be back as soon as I can.

She grabs her keys and her oversized hoodie and disappears out the apartment door.

SCENE TEN (A)

HOLLAND's office on the Luminia Campus. Night. Only the desk lamp is on. It rains heavily outside.

HOLLAND is working to pack some materials into an attaché case. It looks like ASHA's assumption that he might try to flee is correct. A wall safe is open. HOLLAND is transferring its contents to the case. There is a soft noise—maybe footsteps—HOLLAND stops what he's doing to listen. The soft footsteps come closer. There is the faint "beep" of a Luminia key card being tapped. HOLLAND pulls back into the shadows. ASHA opens the door carefully and enters the room. She doesn't see HOLLAND in the shadows. He watches her investigate the room cautiously. She notices the case. She notices the open wall safe. She approaches it cautiously. HOLLAND steps out of the shadows at her back. Preoccupied with the safe, ASHA doesn't hear him approach. With sudden violence, he grabs her, clamping his hand over her mouth. She screams against his palm as she tries to fight him off, but is radically overpowered. The desk lamp crashes to the ground. Darkness.

SCENE TEN (B)

ASHA's apartment. MEDINA has almost freed himself—he's probably had to disassemble the radiator to do it. His phone is ringing loudly. The last piece of the radiator comes loose. He yanks his still-cuffed hands free. He bolts to the counter and grabs the phone.

MEDINA: Medina.

He scrambles. He's trying to talk on the phone while still handcuffed, simultaneously digging out his wallet and rooting through it for the handcuff key he always keeps there.

BEECHUM: It's not Ruiz.

MEDINA stills.

The remains. They're not her.

MEDINA: Are you sure? Sometimes decomposition—
We should wait for a DNA comparison—

BEECHUM: They're skeletonized. Forensics says they've been out here ten *years* minimum.

MEDINA: Can we still link Holland to them?

BEECHUM: Maybe. We ran the dentals and got a missing persons hit. There's a file on a missing girl thought to be connected at the time with a different group that Holland ran.

MEDINA: At the time?

BEECHUM: It's a sixteen-year-old file.

Silence as MEDINA digests this.

There's something else.

MEDINA: What?

BEECHUM: The skeletonized girl? According to the missing persons report, her name is *Asha Ray.*

SCENE TEN (C)

KATE runs down a darkened alleyway, jumping over trash bags and swerving around dumpsters. She slips on the wet street and scrambles back to her feet—heart hammering. She runs until the alleyway merges into the familiar lonely stretch of road under the overpass and the "What Are You Capable Of?" billboard—she slows. She looks around. No one is pursuing her—the street is deserted. She holds her sides, still breathing hard.

SCENE TEN (D)

The Luminia Campus. HOLLAND's office. The police, BEECHUM, and MEDINA have all converged on the scene. They break open the office door. ASHA sits on the ground, leaning against the desk. HOLLAND's body is sprawled out on the floor, his head resting in her lap.

Intermission.

ACT TWO

SCENE ONE

The interview room at the police station—later that night. MEDINA is behind the glass; ASHA sits alone in the interview room. In this light, we see that she's badly banged up. It seems pretty indisputable that she had to fight HOLLAND for her life.

She picks at the paper coffee cup she's been given.

BEECHUM passes through the area where MEDINA waits—she nods to him, but they don't speak.

BEECHUM enters the interview room alone. In addition to her notes and files, she's carrying a microwaveable frozen meal.

BEECHUM: Here.

She passes ASHA the Lean Cuisine.

ASHA: It's frozen.

BEECHUM: It's for your face.

ASHA: No peas?

BEECHUM: It's a police precinct. People around here think ketchup is a vegetable.

ASHA gingerly rests the Lean Cuisine against her swelling cheek and rapidly colouring eye. She flinches a little.

The adrenaline surge she'd had in HOLLAND*'s office has now subsided and she is feeling her injuries.*

Looks painful.

ASHA *looks at her.*

ASHA: You should see the other guy.

BEECHUM*'s lip twitches, but she says nothing.* BEECHUM *takes a seat at the table. She opens her folder.*

BEECHUM: I read over your statement.

Silence.

I've got a few questions.

ASHA: I thought you might.

BEECHUM *slides a piece of paper across the desk to* ASHA*.*

BEECHUM: Do you know what this is?

ASHA *looks at the document, her expression gives nothing away.*

ASHA: Looks like a missing persons report.

BEECHUM: It is.

BEECHUM *watches* ASHA *as she speaks.*

It was filed by a "Sarah Smith." Do you know who that is?

ASHA: Sounds like an alias.

BEECHUM: Sounds like.

It's a standoff.

"Sarah Smith" filed this report with the Flintland Police Department sixteen years ago.

She is described as an *(reading from the report)* "adolescent female"—not a lot to go on.

BEECHUM watches ASHA closely.

In this document, Ms. Smith discloses that she's a member of a private society believed to be operated by a philosophy professor recently returned from California. She describes residing with her "family" in the former dormitories of the Teacher's College out near the Rock Ridge townsite—just down the highway from the Rock Ridge Truck Stop.

She felt compelled to make the report as she believed harm had come to another member of her "family"—another young woman—whom she knew only as "Asha Ray."

She looks directly at ASHA as she says this. ASHA's expression is carefully blank—she knows the content of this missing persons report intimately; nothing BEECHUM has mined from it is surprising to her, though she is perhaps subtly impressed at BEECHUM's obvious skill in connecting the dots.

Ms. Smith described having witnessed a series of disturbing confrontations between the organization's leader—a man whose name she wouldn't disclose—and other young, female members of "the family."

She told the officer taking the report that she was compelled to come to the police after thinking deeply about an incident three nights prior, in which she'd witnessed the man stripping the missing woman's bed—disposing of her personal belongings. He explained simply that Asha had deserted the family, giving other members the directive to "forget her name" and to "never speak it aloud again."

According to the notes made by the case officer, Ms. Smith had ridden her bicycle almost twenty kilometres in the rain along dark highway roads at night to come into the station and make the report. In her statement, Ms. Smith told Officer Paul Kelly that she believed her friend Asha Ray was dead.

A long silence.

ASHA: What happened next?

BEECHUM flips through the file, though she already knows its content inside and out.

BEECHUM: Nothing. Looks like a couple uniforms were dispatched—sent out there to feel it out. Looks like they spoke to the guy. They reported that he seemed like a decent dude—

ASHA: Is that *in* the report?

This is the first flicker of any kind of real reaction from ASHA.

BEECHUM: No. But it might as well be, right?

ASHA gets herself back under control.

The note just says that everything seemed above board when they visited the "campus." It says that they were given a tour, and that the guy running the show explained that he was basically a good Samaritan—providing room, board, and jobs to disenfranchised young people who'd burned their other bridges.

ASHA has slipped back behind her wall of composure. She gives no reaction to this information.

And then . . . nothing. No follow up. No return visit. The original case officer, Paul Kelly, did some digging on the alleged victim; but outside of dental records and a partial juvie sheet, he wasn't able to turn up much—looks like the kid had been a runaway. She didn't have anyone out there missing her.

BEECHUM looks intently at ASHA again. ASHA doesn't respond.

Sixteen years ago you filed a request to legally change your name to Asha Ray . . . from Sarah Daniels. Is that correct?

ASHA: Yes.

BEECHUM taps the missing persons report.

BEECHUM: Did you file this? Sixteen years ago?

Silence.

Because that was smart. "Sarah Smith" was smart. And brave. She took a lot of personal risk to try and get justice for someone else. I respect that.

Silence.

BEECHUM opens a different folder.

In your statement, you wrote that you went to Richard Holland's office this evening in order to prevent him from evading justice, is that correct?

ASHA: Yes.

BEECHUM: You believed Mr. Holland would be endeavouring to flee impending, undisclosed charges against him.

ASHA: Yes.

BEECHUM: You wrote that you were advised of these *impending* charges by a consulting colleague, is that correct?

> *ASHA hesitates half a fraction. Her gaze flicks to the two-way mirror where she assumes (correctly) that MEDINA is listening.*

ASHA: Yes.

BEECHUM: And you believed the information to be credible?

ASHA: Yes.

BEECHUM: Why?

ASHA: My consultant is a decorated and respected retired law enforcement officer.

BEECHUM: You are referring to Mr. Reuben Medina.

ASHA: Yes.

BEECHUM: Was Mr. Medina aware of your intention to confront Richard Holland?

ASHA: No. I never said where I was going.

BEECHUM: But you departed his company immediately after the subject of impending charges against Holland was discussed.

ASHA: Yes.

BEECHUM: And Mr. Medina chose not to pursue you?

ASHA: No.

BEECHUM: Why not?

ASHA: He was handcuffed to a radiator.

A stunned pause.

BEECHUM: He—what?

ASHA: I had handcuffed Mr. Medina to the radiator in my apartment. So that he couldn't follow me.

BEECHUM is stunned and trying hard to mask her amusement.

BEECHUM: I'm sorry, you *overpowered* Mr. Medina and *physically* detained him to prevent him pursuing you when you went to confront Richard Holland.

ASHA: Yes. Further, I ensured his phone was removed from his person, so that he couldn't notify law enforcement of my intentions.

BEECHUM: What were your intentions?

ASHA: I intended to stop Richard Holland from fleeing before charges could be brought against him.

BEECHUM: How? You're not law enforcement—how did you hope to legally detain Mr. Holland.

ASHA: I aimed to persuade him to change course—to behave honourably and accept the consequences of his actions with grace.

BEECHUM looks skeptical.

BEECHUM: You broke into the man's office in order to speak with him?

ASHA: That's what I've testified to in my written statement, yes.

BEECHUM: And, what? If things got dicey, you planned to handcuff him to a radiator?

ASHA: I had no plan to physically engage Mr. Holland.

BEECHUM: No. Of course you didn't.

Pause.

You could have reported your suspicions.

ASHA: To whom?

BEECHUM: The police?

ASHA: The police who believed they had Richard Holland "under surveillance" at his home at the time he was across town at his office packing all his valuables into a suitcase?

Silence.

BEECHUM: What happened?

ASHA: It's in the report.

BEECHUM: I'd like you to go over it for me.

Silence.

ASHA: He grabbed me.

A pause. She exhales.

I opened his office door. It was dark—just the desk light on. It seemed empty. I saw the suitcase, the wall safe open—I crossed the space to investigate the contents of the case. Holland was there—behind me.

He grabbed me.

She looks ill.

BEECHUM: Then what?

ASHA shakes her head.

ASHA: I don't know. I fought back, I guess. I remember biting his hand. I got in some swings, maybe. He hit my head against the desk *(touches her own cheek)*. He was trying to choke me, crush me. I just thought . . . I was thinking I was going to die . . . and I just thought NO. Not like this. Not this man. Not like this.

BEECHUM: You broke his neck.

ASHA: He would have killed me.

Silence settles in the room. Neither BEECHUM nor ASHA moves.

On the other side of the glass, MEDINA suddenly leaves the room.

SCENE TWO (A)

An underground subway station, late afternoon the same day. KATE *arrives, carrying a backpack. It's still raining above ground, the floors down here are slick. Her hood is up. She scopes the place out. She looks around for other passengers. The place is deserted. She sets up her phone as a camera on a ledge. She walks away from it, moving toward the edge of the platform—she walks past the safety line. She takes down her hood. She stares into the darkness of the subway tunnel. The phone flashes—it has taken an incognito photo. She walks back over to the camera and picks it up. She checks the image she captured—it is of her on the platform, face turned most of the way toward the camera, station signage visible behind her. She texts something. She puts the phone back in her pocket. She pulls her hood back up and leaves the subway station.*

SCENE TWO (B)

The LANGDON *family home—a Georgian style mansion on the corner lot of a gated community—late afternoon the same day.* MATT *Langdon lays on his bed in the dark, curtains drawn, the rain is still coming down heavily outside. There is a buzz and a blue glow from the nightstand.* MATT *picks up his phone. He looks at the message. He sits up.*

SCENE THREE

ASHA's apartment, late afternoon the same day. MEDINA is just finishing repairing ASHA's deadbolt—she's not home. MEDINA's phone rings, he picks it up.

MEDINA: Medina.

BEECHUM: Is she with you?

MEDINA: Who? Asha?

BEECHUM: Yeah.

MEDINA: No.

Pause.

She's not at the station? You released her?

BEECHUM: No. I had her waiting at my desk—in central booking.

MEDINA: And?

BEECHUM: She walked out.

MEDINA: She—how?

BEECHUM's annoyance is palpable through the phone.

BEECHUM: It *appears* she asked someone where she could

microwave her lunch. He showed her to a breakroom, and she threw that damned Lean Cuisine on high for four minutes. Her escort left her there, and she walked out the front door.

Pause.

MEDINA: Sounds about right.

BEECHUM: Where are you now?

Pause.

MEDINA: I'm at her apartment.

BEECHUM: Medina.

Pause.

MEDINA: She hasn't been back.

Pause.

I'm fixing her lock.

Pause.

BEECHUM: We're sending a unit to stake out the place. They'll be over in twenty minutes.

She has a lot of thoughts. She chooses not to voice any of them.

Don't still be there.

She hangs up.

MEDINA stands. He realizes one of ASHA's neighbours is watching him from the hallway. SERGE approaches MEDINA. He is older—maybe in his sixties, but he looks to have lived a hard life, so it's difficult to say. He speaks with a heavy Russian accent. SERGE leans against the door jamb.

SERGE: You cop?

MEDINA: No.

SERGE looks MEDINA over. He narrows his eyes.

SERGE: You look like *cop.*

Pause.

I tell her, I say: There is cop. He fix door.

MEDINA: Tell . . . her?

SERGE: Asha. I tell her.

MEDINA: Just now?

SERGE: Da.

MEDINA: She's here?

SERGE: No. On telephone. She say: Serge? Look my apartment.
There are cops?
I say: Da.

MEDINA: You have a number? A phone number?

SERGE: No. Not for you. *Cop.*

MEDINA: Listen . . .

SERGE: Serge.

MEDINA: Serge. I really need to speak with Asha. I'm a good cop. I'm a friend.

SERGE: Heh. *Good cop?* Svolach!

He spits on the ground—whether to punctuate his statement or just-because is unclear.

She say: no number for cop. Only message.

MEDINA: Message?

SERGE: Da.

MEDINA: What's the message?

SERGE: Best of West. Dogs. Seventy-six dogs.

MEDINA blinks at him.

MEDINA: Thanks, Serge.

MEDINA grabs his jacket and tools. He locks up ASHA's place and races from the apartment.

MEDINA runs on foot through the rainy city again as darkness settles. Everything feels more intense now—the traffic, the light of the reflected billboard lights, the screech and hiss of traffic, the thrumming rumble of the subway. By the time MEDINA reaches Franco's Franks, he's soaked. He approaches FRANCO.

Excuse me, there's a message here for me?

FRANCO blinks at him.

FRANCO: What are you talking about, a message?

MEDINA: A note.

FRANCO: Buddy, this is a hot dog cart, not a goddamned girls locker room.

MEDINA's face falls.

HA! Just yanking your chain. Here you go, pal.

He passes MEDINA a folded-up napkin.

You want a dog for the road? Best dogs west of / West 76th.

MEDINA: / West 76th. I know. Yeah. Sure. Dog me.

MEDINA takes the napkin and the hot dog. He starts eating the dog, unfolding the napkin to read it as he goes. He almost collides with BEECHUM who plants herself in his path.

BEECHUM: Medina.

He blinks at her. She gestures for him to follow her to the shelter offered by the awning of a bodega.

MEDINA: You tailing me now?

She spots the writing on the napkin.

BEECHUM: Is that an address?

MEDINA: No.

He hands her the napkin. She looks at it. She turns it around. It's a drawing—a simple map—but the details are too vague for BEECHUM *to be able to make sense of it.*

BEECHUM: You know where this is?

He continues eating the hot dog.

MEDINA: Walk away.

BEECHUM: Excuse me?

MEDINA: I'm asking you to walk away.

Silence.

BEECHUM: What's going on?

MEDINA: I don't know.

BEECHUM: Bullshit.

MEDINA: Asha—

BEECHUM: Killed a man.

Pause.

She killed a man, Reuben.

Pause.

MEDINA: How does a *fuck-up* like that happen?
How does a guy under suspicion in a woman's death—supposedly

under surveillance—slip his detail and end up halfway across the city without anyone fucking noticing?

Silence.

BEECHUM: What are you asking me?

MEDINA: I want to know why you flinched.

BEECHUM: Flinched?

MEDINA: Backed off him.

BEECHUM: *Backed off him?* I drove out to the damned end of the earth to show his picture around a truck stop—I spent all day out in a marsh with a cadaver team on the off chance we might get something to nail the guy with. I did not *back off him.*

MEDINA: I read the report. Only one unit—two rookies—all the way up the block.

BEECHUM: You think I was *letting* him run?

MEDINA: I think you were playing politic instead of doing your job.

Silence.

BEECHUM: I made a call.

MEDINA: It was the wrong call.

BEECHUM: Sometimes we make the wrong call.

MEDINA: No. You don't get to make the wrong call. Ever. You definitely don't get to make the wrong call because some asshole with more stripes is breathing down your neck. That's the job.

BEECHUM: There's a hierarchy, Medina.
A goddamned chain of command.
That is the job.

MEDINA: The second you let obedience outweigh your better judgment, you're done. Walk away. Not just from this case. *Walk away.*

Trying to fix the game, while still playing the fucking game, will eat you alive.

Trust me.

He finishes eating his hot dog. He leaves her standing under the awning.

SCENE FOUR

The Clairmont. Night. The diner is closed. ASHA *waits inside for* MEDINA. *When he arrives, she unlocks the door and lets him in. She locks the door behind him.*

ASHA: I need your help.

He stares at her in hurt disbelief.

MEDINA: You do, huh?

He looks around, simmering.

You steal the key to this place off a line cook out back having a smoke, or you just hide out somewhere during regular business hours and then come out after everyone has gone home?

ASHA: I own it.

Whatever he expected, this wasn't it.

My apartment is under surveillance.

MEDINA: Because you fled a police station after being lawfully detained for killing a man.

ASHA: I had something I had to do.

She looks at MEDINA *intently. A buzzing silence.*

Maya Ruiz is missing.

MEDINA: What are you talking about?

ASHA: Maya Ruiz is alive—and she's missing.

The buzzing seems to intensify.

She survived her attack. When she was dumped in the park—she was still alive. Barely. She regained consciousness. She was hypothermic, badly injured, and disoriented, but alive.

MEDINA radiates an intensity it's hard to place—fury? Relief? He rubs his face. Emotion crashes over him like a wave. He sits. ASHA sits opposite him.

She spent three days out in the woods—got picked up walking along the highway, wrapped in a blue throw—asked to be taken to a shelter.

That's when her case was brought to my attention.

A slight pause.

Ten days ago.

The betrayal this admission implies hangs in the space between them

I got here—after I left the police station—and I found this.

She takes the envelope and nametag reading "KATE" that Maya had left on the counter of the Clairmont when locking up the night before. She sets them on the table.

ASHA: It just says thank you, and that she's sorry.

. . . and that there's something she's got to do.

MEDINA: Doesn't feel great, does it?

ASHA: No.

MEDINA: You think she means Langdon?

ASHA: Yes.

MEDINA: Are you sure?

ASHA hesitates a fraction.

ASHA: You know her better than I do.

MEDINA: Is that why I'm here, then?

ASHA: I trust you.

And—obviously—I can't involve the police.

MEDINA: *You trust me?* I don't even know where to *start* with *that.*

He stands.

ASHA: I do. I trust you.

MEDINA: Well I don't trust you. I don't trust this. I am tired too, *Asha.*
I'm tired of the head games and the bullshit and the notes and the calculated *moves* and never knowing what the fuck is really going on.

I was *grieving* for that girl.

You *knew* that. You *saw* that.

And you just sat there, letting me pull my own guts out over it—

ASHA: That's the job.

MEDINA: WHAT job? What job are you talking about? The job where you impersonate cult members? Bust into office buildings? Or the job where you run an unauthorized witness protection program out the back door of a *fucking* diner?

Silence.

ASHA: I'm not going to defend myself to you.

Silence.

I would have told you. About Maya. Later, when—

MEDINA: When what?

ASHA: When she was situated. When she was safe.

MEDINA: You risked her life. By not bringing her to the police. By not getting her real protection. By not having her *press charges* against Matt Langdon—seek a restraining order, whatever. If she'd gone to the police with her evidence, her testimony, instead of skulking off in secret, Matt Langdon would be—

ASHA: At home.
Matt Langdon would *still* be at home.
But he'd know Maya Ruiz was alive.
And out there somewhere waiting to testify against him.

I told her she was better off staying dead.
Safer.

I told her that challenging those men in court was a gamble—one with bad odds for her. The probability that Matt Langdon would dispute her account and plead his charges down to misdemeanor assault was decent.

I convinced her to look after herself, first.

MEDINA: Meaning what?

ASHA: Meaning lay low until it's safe and then walk away. Start over. Start over with *no one* looking for her. Let them get away with it. Let them plant the car. Let them tell the story that Maya Ruiz must have just skipped town.

MEDINA: What happened?

ASHA: Matt Langdon is not a great criminal. He's cocky and he's sloppy. The police were suspicious, they were digging. And Kelly was digging. And *you* were digging. It was only a matter of time before someone dug up a lead—got a tip from the motorist who'd picked up the girl in the blue throw walking along the highway—something.

MEDINA: So . . . then?

ASHA: We changed strategy.

Pause.

I asked Paul Kelly to refer me to Grant Langdon.

MEDINA: Why?

ASHA: I thought—if I could get to Matt Langdon—I could flip him. Turn him against Holland. Pit them against each other. Have him testify to Holland's involvement to cut a deal. Then it becomes a matter of legal record that Maya Ruiz is dead—people stop looking. Maybe there are even some consequences for Langdon and Holland.

There's a sudden chilliness.

MEDINA: How did you think you would get to him?
Matt Langdon was in police custody.
How did you think you were going to get to talk to him?

She understands what he's asking.

ASHA: I'm resourceful. I make the most of my circumstance—

MEDINA: Is that what I am? A circumstance? You knew I was coming over—

ASHA: You called. You left that message. I hadn't thought to involve you, but then—

MEDINA: Your door.

Silence.

You kicked in your fucking door. Why?

Silence.

ASHA: You were looking for her. You weren't going to stop, unless—

MEDINA: Unless?

ASHA: I thought, if I could shift your focus to me, if *I* needed you . . .

MEDINA: I would feel compelled to help you? Protect you? Do whatever you asked me to do?

ASHA: Yes.

A blistering silence.

MEDINA: You . . . you just know *exactly* what buttons to push, don't you?

ASHA: It's the / job—

MEDINA: / Do NOT say it's the fucking job.

The air between them throbs. ASHA is unsure if MEDINA will simply storm out. He's probably thinking about it.

ASHA: I'm sorry.

For what it's worth.

I'm sorry.

MEDINA says nothing.

MEDINA: Why do you think she abandoned the plan?

ASHA: Yesterday—I told her about Matt. About the plea.

MEDINA: And?

ASHA: And she was furious. I talked her down, but—

MEDINA: But later, when you turned your back, she bolted—probably to go do something exceptionally dangerous.

Sounds familiar.

ASHA: Except—

MEDINA: Except she doesn't have the skills to protect herself *when* things go sideways.

Silence.

ASHA: Are you going to help?

MEDINA: I'd have to be a real heartless prick not to, wouldn't I?

MEDINA radiates fury. ASHA seems tired.

You got any leads?

ASHA: No.

MEDINA: Matt Langdon can't leave his home.

ASHA: Matt Langdon is a wealthy sociopath. We can't assume he's still at home. Not if he doesn't want to be.

MEDINA: You think she lured him out?

ASHA: It's what I would do.

MEDINA: How?

ASHA: I don't know.

MEDINA: What would you do?

ASHA: *I don't know*. Show up? Look around? See what struck me?

MEDINA: Does she have a phone? I know *her* phone is in evidence, but—

ASHA: She has a burner.

Well, not a real burner. It's an old phone of mine. I keep it and a laptop here, so they can contact me. The GPS function is disabled, if that's what you're thinking.

MEDINA: It wasn't.

Pause. He thinks about it.

Is that phone still connected to your cloud?

ASHA: My . . . what?

MEDINA: Where does its data backup go?

ASHA just blinks at him.

ASHA: Since when are you a cyber sleuth?

MEDINA: Knowing about the existence of the cloud isn't cyber sleuthing. Where's the laptop?

ASHA digs it out from under the till. MEDINA opens it.

It was backed up earlier today. We might be able to see what was sent.

ASHA is stunned.

ASHA: You think she texted him?

MEDINA: It's worth a shot.

MEDINA works quickly.

Got it. Outgoing text at 4:06 p.m. We'd have to check the message number is Langdon's, but I feel that's a safe bet.

ASHA: What does it say?

MEDINA calls up the message.

MEDINA: It's a photo. Look.

ASHA does.

ASHA: It's her face.

MEDINA: It's her, alive, at a subway station, taken today.

ASHA is shocked.

He shows this to anyone, and he'll walk. All charges dropped. What's she doing?

ASHA: She's betting he won't. She's betting he'll come himself.

MEDINA: There's text underneath. It says:

Seen her every night this week.
M Train.
North platform at Dalwood & 72nd.
9 p.m.

Always in the light.

ASHA: She's making him think the message is from a friend—a Luminia member tipping him off. *Always in the light.*

What time is it?

MEDINA: Almost nine.

They look at each other. ASHA grabs her keys off the counter.

SCENE FIVE

The subway station at Dalwood & 72nd. Underground. The sounds of trains shrieking and rumbling through dozens of tunnels. Flickering darkness and light. KATE/MAYA *waits alone on the northbound platform. She wears a hoodie and chucks. She looks younger than her age. She has nothing on her—no backpack, no weapons. She stands on the yellow line, toward the centre of the platform. She stares ahead. No one else is around.* MATT *arrives on the platform. He's dressed in dark jeans, and a jacket with a hood.*

MATT: Maya.

MAYA *turns around. She looks frightened, frozen. A deer in headlights.*

I didn't mean to. Maya, I didn't.

MAYA: Didn't mean to? Didn't mean to *what*? Strangle me? Wrap me up in an afghan my grandmother knitted and throw me in the trunk of my car? Drive me out to the woods then dump my body in a storm drain? What part did you not mean to do?

MATT *takes a step toward her.*

Fuck you. Don't come near me.

MATT: I got in my head.
About you.
About us.

I just—
It was eating me, you know.
I just wanted—
You weren't answering.
I came over because you weren't answering.
And then you—when you came home—you weren't even sorry

ASHA and MEDINA have arrived—they stick to the shadows. They split up, edging closer to MATT and MAYA from different sides.

MAYA: Stay back.

MATT: Maya—
Just listen to me—
I didn't want to hurt you—

MAYA: You were waiting. In my apartment. In the dark.

MATT: I was just—I needed to think—

MAYA: Think about what?

MATT: What I should do.
How to help you.
I still want to help you.
Only now—I think we can help each other—

He takes another step toward her.

MAYA: I won't help you.

There is a low rumble deep in the tunnel. Something shifts in MATT.

MATT: He was right about you.

Richard.
He was right.
He said you weren't worth the trouble.

MAYA: You called him. You asked him where to take me.

MATT: He said: "Don't worry. She won't be missed. That girl has no one."

> *There is the loud shriek of metal—a deep rumbling. A train is approaching.* MATT *takes another step forward. In a flash, it's very clear what he plans to do.* MAYA *seems paralyzed as he moves toward her.*

MATT: Such a WASTE.

> *He shoves* MAYA *hard, intending to push her directly into the path of the oncoming train. In that instant, the following:* ASHA *and* MEDINA *both lunge for* MATT *and* MAYA*, but they are both too far to close the distance.* MAYA *has anticipated the shove, grabbing* MATT*'s shirt and pulling him down with her. For a terrifying moment, it looks like they've both gone down in front of the train. There is a screaming metallic noise.* MATT *and* MAYA *didn't go over the edge—they are both on the lip of the platform, locked in a physical altercation.* MATT *is overpowering* MAYA*.* MEDINA *reaches the pair before* ASHA*. He hauls* MATT *off* MAYA *and physically subdues him.*

> *The lights of the subway station flicker.* MEDINA *looks up at* MAYA *and* ASHA *from the ground where he has* MATT *pinned. They all just breathe for a moment.* MAYA *goes over to the ledge where her phone is resting. She collects it. She gives it to* ASHA*.* ASHA *digs into her pocket. She takes out the diner keys. She gives both* MAYA*'s phone and the diner keys to* MEDINA*.*

ASHA: Here. This is everything you'll need.

He looks at the keys.

MEDINA: What's this?

ASHA: These are for the diner. I'm heading out of town for a bit.

MEDINA: What do you mean you're—Asha!

She starts to leave. MEDINA *wants to chase after her, but he needs to restrain* MATT.

ARE YOU SERIOUS? ASHA.

ASHA *and* MAYA *both zip up their oversized hoodies and leave the station together.*

In the foreground, MEDINA *works to restrain* MATT *as he watches them exit together—looking strikingly alike with their hoods up—a realization dawns on him:*

A reprise: ASHA*'s confrontation with* HOLLAND*. The scene is how we originally experienced it, only this time it plays out as follows:*

Night. The Luminia Campus. HOLLAND*'s office. The space appears empty—illuminated only by the desk light. The wall safe and attaché case are open.* HOLLAND *packs. There is a soft sound from down the hall, possibly footsteps.* HOLLAND *retreats into the shadows. There is the "beep" of a Luminia key card.* ASHA *enters the room, hood up. She leaves the office door ajar. She spots the open case and wall safe and crosses the room.* HOLLAND *emerges from the shadows, closing in on* ASHA *from behind. He grabs her, his hand over her mouth. In this action, the hood of* ASHA*'s jacket slips* *down revealing the figure to be* MAYA. *She screams, but the palm of his hand muffles it. They struggle. The desk light crashes to the floor, the only light source now is the light from the hallway. The door to the office opens wider.* ASHA *appears in the doorway. She gets the drop on* HOLLAND, *as he is distracted by the struggling* MAYA. HOLLAND *lets go of* MAYA *to fight* ASHA. *He throws* ASHA *into the desk.* MAYA *tries to pull him off* ASHA. HOLLAND *rounds on* MAYA. ASHA *gets her arm around his neck and, in a smooth, brutal movement, breaks it.* HOLLAND *slumps to the floor.* MAYA *goes to* ASHA *and they hold onto each other for a couple moments before* ASHA *nods for* MAYA *to leave the office.*

End of play.

ACKNOWLEDGEMENTS

I would like to gratefully acknowledge the contributions made to this play by the artists, crew, and staff of Vertigo Theatre, as well as the organizational and creative teams that supported development workshops and public readings of this play in Alberta and British Columbia. I would like to further acknowledge the support and encouragement of the following individuals: Craig Hall, Jenna Rodgers, KP Smith, Laurel Green, Devin MacKinnon, Lori Sobkowich, Don Smith, and Dave, Karen, Daniel, Kelk, and Lucy Jeffery.

Michaela Jeffery is an award-winning Calgary-based playwright and graduate of the National Theatre School of Canada. Selected writing credits include *The Extractionist*, WROL *(Without Rule of Law)*, *Wolf on the Ringstrasse*, *The Listening Room*, *Godhead*, and *Always*. She has been a finalist for ATHE's Jane Chambers Playwriting Award for excellence in feminist theatre, the Alberta Playwrights' Network's Alberta Playwriting Competition, and the Playwrights Guild of Canada's RBC Emerging Playwright Award.